OSPREY
PUBLISHING

The German Army 1914–18

D S V Fosten & R J Marrion • Illustrated by G A Embleton

Series editor Martin Windrow

First published in Great Britain in 1978 by
Osprey Publishing, Midland House, West Way,
Botley, Oxford OX2 0PH, UK
443 Park Avenue South, New York, NY 10016, USA
Email: info@ospreypublishing.com

© 1978 Osprey Publishing Ltd.
Reprinted 1981, 1982 (twice), 1984, 1985, 1986, 1987
(twice), 1988, 1989, 1991, 1992, 1994, 1995, 1996,
1997, 1998, 1999, 2002 (twice), 2003, 2004, 2005

ISBN 0 85045 283 x

CIP Data for this publication is available from
the British Library

Series Editor: MARTIN WINDROW

Filmset in Great Britain
Printed in China through World Print Ltd.

FOR A CATALOGUE OF ALL BOOKS PUBLISHED BY
OSPREY MILITARY AND AVIATION PLEASE CONTACT:

NORTH AMERICA
Osprey Direct, 2427 Bond Street,
University Park, IL 60466, USA
E-mail: info@ospreydirectusa.com

ALL OTHER REGIONS
Osprey Direct UK, P.O. Box 140, Wellingborough,
Northants, NN8 2FA, UK
E-mail: info@ospreydirect.co.uk

www.ospreypublishing.com

The Unification of Germany

In 1870–1 Prussia, allied with Bavaria and other German states, defeated the French. In January 1871 the North German Federation was dissolved, giving way to the German Empire or 'Reich', with King William I of Prussia as the first Emperor. In a remarkably short time Prussia, under the guidance of Otto von Bismarck, Helmuth von Moltke and Albrecht von Roon, fashioned an Empire with a constitution which was to serve it well until the abdication of the Kaiser in 1918. The most important factor of this formidable union, from the point of view of the European balance of power, was the formation of a powerful German Army.

The father of the new army was Helmuth Karl Bernhard, Graf von Moltke (1800–91).* An avid student of the theories of Clausewitz and Gneisenau, he entered military service as a cadet in the Danish Army in 1811, but later resigned his commission to enter Prussian service. In 1858, after a richly varied career, this brilliant officer was appointed Chief of the General Staff to the Prussian Army; and for the rest of his life he devoted most of his talents to the formation, instruction, and evolution of that Staff and of the Army it was to direct with such superb professionalism.

The new army consisted of contingents from twenty-six states, four kingdoms, five grand duchies, twelve duchies and principalities, three free cities, and Alsace-Lorraine. Moltke conceived the nucleus as the Prussian Army with its elaborate established structure headed by the Military Cabinet, supported by the War Ministry and

General Staff. The lower staff echelons included Inspectorates of the various Arms and Services and a plethora of Officer Academies and NCO Schools. The Armies of Saxony and Württemberg also retained their War Ministries, General Staffs, Inspectorates and Establishments; while the Armies of the Grand Duchies of Hess and Mecklenberg retained many of their old characteristics as self-standing contingents, though under the aegis of Prussia.

Two NCOs of the 20th Ulan Regiment, 2nd Württemberg, König Wilhelm. Both are wearing the field-grey lancer uniform with special pear-shaped shoulder straps.

---

* Not to be confused with Helmuth Johannes Ludwig von Moltke, 1848–1916, subsequent Chief of the German General Staff, who succeeded von Schlieffen. He was Generalissimo of the Army in October 1914 when, following the failure of the great plan to destroy the French Army in Champagne, he resigned and was replaced by von Falkenhayn.

A group of Landsturm of Landsturm Battalion No. 42, part of the X Army Corps District garrisoned in Wetzlar, between Kassel and Frankfurt. They are wearing the dark blue 'Bluse' and Jäger shako with a large white Landwehr Cross in an oval on the front. The Arabic unit designation and Army Corps number in Roman numerals is worn on either side of the collar front. All carry obsolete rifles and bayonets.

The Kingdom of Bavaria provided the next largest contingent, and her three Army Corps were almost completely autonomous. The large Bavarian General Staff and War Ministry had headquarters at Munich and were supported by large Inspectorates, Officer Academies and NCO Schools modelled on the Prussian pattern. Officers of Saxon and Bavarian Army Corps were on separate promotion lists, although Prussian and Württemberg officers were interchangeable. Between 1880 and 1914 Moltke's brilliantly organized General Staff, with its hard core of professional Prussian Junker senior officers, moulded this loosely structured mass of units into a tightly knit fighting machine, highly trained and educated in all the technical skills of the art of war.

There is no place here for a survey of the political events which led up to the outbreak of the First World War. At 8pm on 1 August 1914 German troops violated the neutrality of Luxembourg; on the same day Germany declared war on Russia, and on 2 August German troops crossed the frontier into France. On the 3rd, Germany declared war on France, and at midnight on the 4th

war was declared between Germany and Great Britain.

The Schlieffen Plan

The plan, conceived by von Moltke, and subsequently developed by Albrecht, Graf von Schlieffen when he succeeded Moltke as Chief of the German General Staff, laid down a strategy to fight on two fronts and yet still finish the war quickly. One Army of four Corps was left in East Prussia to contain any initial Russian advance and to co-operate with the Austrians, who were to attack through Poland. Austria was to withdraw some troops from her front with Serbia to develop a strike at Russia through Galicia. The main German force was to attack France, striking through Belgium, move quickly into the department of Champagne, smash the French in one great battle, isolate Paris, then roll the remains of the French Army up to the Swiss border. Behind this massive advance by first-rate Active Army Corps through Belgium, reserve formations were to rush to the Channel ports to prevent the British uniting with the French.

However, the gallant resistance of the Belgians and outnumbered French slowed down the German advance, and unexpectedly strong Russian advances in East Prussia necessitated two additional Army Corps being detached from the West to the East. The depleted German force fighting the

4

Belgians and the Franco-British thus no longer had the necessary impetus to achieve its original objectives and, between 6 and 10 September, the Franco-British Army fought them to a standstill at the Battle for the Marne. The defeated Germans were not routed, but fell back in good order to positions north of the Aisne which they fortified and held. It was in this sector of the Western Front that trench warfare started.

Trench Warfare

After the Battle of the Marne, sectors of the Western Front developed a type of siege warfare which, as the war progressed, spread over much of the 500 miles of front from the Swiss border to the sea. Elaborate systems were devised to protect troops fighting from static positions often only a hundred yards apart. Complicated trench systems were reinforced with sandbags, revetted with timber and sometimes steel or concrete. Some were shallow, others deep enough to protect a standing man. Trenches were divided into sections by means of traverses, or made serpentine or zig-zag according to local requirements. Dug-out shelters were provided at intervals to act as command posts, shelters during bombardments, and dressing stations. Most trenches had firing steps, firing positions for snipers and fixed periscope positions, while others had steel-plate reinforcement with loopholes along the parapets. In front of the trenches there were mazes of barbed wire which were often as much as 100ft deep, and behind them support and communication trenches, along which relieving or reinforcing troops could be moved up.

Under appalling conditions, massive numbers of infantry moving over open ground fought ferocious battles in the face of massed artillery and machine guns to gain limited success, often fighting hand-to-hand over only a few yards of blood-soaked ground. Before the war was over hundreds of thousands of men were to die without either side gaining any positive advantage.

Other Theatres

Prior to the Armistice the German Army was to fight, not only on the Western Front, but in Russia, the Balkans and Italy. German soldiers also served alongside the Turks in Asia Minor and small contingents fought the Japanese at Kiao Chau in Eastern China, defended the Caroline and Marshall Islands, and served in Samoa, New Guinea, and in Africa. Although German garrisons and their native levies in West and South-West Africa and in some parts of the Cameroons were defeated early in the war, in East Africa the main contingent of Schutztruppen and native *askaris* under Lettow-

Ulan patrol in full marching order. Note the pear-shaped shoulder straps and tschapska covers.

Vorbeck fought well and proved difficult to subdue. In November 1918 he still had 1,500 active German troops and levies under his command. Still under arms they crossed the border into northern Rhodesia and finally surrendered in accordance with Armistice conditions, later returning to Germany with honour. In Russia most of the fighting was more open and mobile than on the Western Front and greater use was made of the cavalry. In Italy and the Balkans specialized mountain jäger, machine gun and ski troops were employed together with mule-drawn mountain artillery.

The Decline of Germany

By the end of 1916 the British blockade was biting deep. Germany had already experienced massive losses in materials and horses, whilst casualty lists grew longer every day. Food was so short that in some areas people were starving. By 1917, although the armies in the field were still doing well, the country as a whole was in economic difficulties. Politically Germany was moving to the left, and the Kaiser was losing much of his former prestige. Raw materials to sustain the war effort were now so short that the War Ministry began to get desperate. Counter-attacks by the reinforced armies in the West had some initial success, but the entry of America into the war was a severe blow and the army on the Western Front began a retreat back into the Hindenburg Line.

Many politicians realized that it was hopeless to continue the war, and on 1 October 1918 even Ludendorff urged the Government to seek peace. Prince Max of Baden, a moderate, was appointed Chancellor and sought negotiations with President Wilson. The British, French and Americans pushed the Germans back; Cambrai, Laon, Roulers, Menin, Ostend, Zeebrugge, Lille, Doudi, Valenciennes, Mons were all rapidly liberated, and on 4 November the Americans captured Sedan. Hindenburg told the Kaiser that he could no longer look to the Army for support if he wished to continue the war. The Kaiser finally abdicated and crossed the border into Holland. The Armistice was signed at 5am on 11 November 1918: the war was over. But discontent among the junior ranks had begun to take hold. On 28 October 1918 a naval mutiny had broken out at Wilhelmshaven and spread rapidly to Kiel; officers were murdered

A Landwehr private dressed for cold weather. Over his normal greatcoat he wears a rabbitskin coat with fur on the inside. The shako has a white cover.

trying to protect their ships. In Germany some army depot battalions mutinied; others formed revolutionary cells, and mobs began to fight in the streets.

The General Staff now had its last momentous task to undertake as part of the Armistice conditions. They had to remove nearly two million men from the Western Front within two weeks, and it says much for their efficiency that this was achieved without serious problems. Soon, roads back to the Fatherland were filled with marching columns. Tired, bitter, hungry and sickened by the massive slaughter, but still considering themselves unbeaten in battle, the German Army went home. Some regiments were headed by their bands, others marched with colours flying, and many men tied oak leaves in their caps. As the weary columns reached German villages and towns men simply walked out of the columns and disappeared into the crowds. Stories began to spread that they had been 'stabbed in the back' by politicians at home. Whole regiments dissolved as men left their units and went home to their families, never to return.

Nine apparently loyal battalions of infantry were rushed to Berlin where naval units had occupied a royal palace, but these never arrived: the men dispersed into the city as they progressed. Soldiers soon began to appear on the streets wearing red brassards and cockades.

Finally the so-called Spartacist Revolt broke out and some of the remaining loyal troops were formed into 'Freikorps'—volunteer units dedicated to maintaining order and preventing a left-wing take-over. Small, but efficient, they smashed riots, kept order in the streets, protected public buildings, and became a mainstay of law and order, although often accused by the left of brutality and excesses. The 'Freikorps', dissolved by order of the Treaty of Versailles, succeeded in preventing Germany becoming a Bolshevik State and eventually many of their members became the first cadres of the subsequent National Socialist Workers Party. During the course of World War I it was estimated that the Germany Army had lost a total of 1,600,000 dead.

The Ausmarsch, 1914

The mobilized German Army fielded the following regiments in August 1914:

5 Regiments of Prussian Foot Guards
4 Regiments of Prussian Guard Grenadiers
1 Prussian Guard Fusilier Regiment
12 Line Grenadier Regiments
182 Infantry and Fusilier Line Regiments
24 Bavarian Infantry Regiments one of which
　　was the Life Regiment
15 Jäger Battalions including the Prussian
　　Guard Schützen Battalion
2 Prussian Guard Machine Gun Detachments
9 Line Machine Gun Detachments including one
　　Saxon and one Bavarian unit
15 Fortress Machine Gun Detachments
10 Kürassier Regiments including a Prussian
　　Guard Regiment and the Prussian
　　Gardes du Corps

3 Saxon Cavalry Regiments including the
　　Guard Regiment
2 Bavarian Heavy Cavalry Regiments
26 Dragoon Regiments including two Prussian
　　Guard Regiments
8 Bavarian Regiments of Light Horse
21 Hussar Regiments including the Prussian
　　Life Guards, 2 Life Regiments and
　　3 Saxon Regiments
23 Lancer Regiments including Prussian Guard
　　Regiments and 1 Saxon and 2 Bavarian
　　Regiments
13 Mounted Rifle Regiments
　　plus Active Guard and Line Artillery,
　　Engineer, Pioneer, Train, Air Service, Signal,
　　Medical and Veterinary Support units
113 Reserve Infantry Regiments
96 Landwehr Infantry Regiments
86 Battalions of Ersatz Infantry
21 Battalions of Landwehr Ersatz Infantry.

Senior NCO of the Württemberg Mountain Battalion. This was a specially raised wartime unit which in May 1918 gained the status of a regiment. There are a number of special features to be noted: the Eidelweiss badge on the cap, the distinctive green patch on either side of the collar, and the green rolls of cloth on each shoulder (just visible on the right shoulder in the photograph). An unusual feature is the NCO's lace, which edges the collar patch and not the front edge of the collar as normal. The small button on the patch bears the company number. The front and bottom of the collar are also piped with green. (W. Y. Carman Collection)

In addition, each Army Corps had squadrons of Reserve Cavalry who were formed into regiments on mobilization and added to Ersatz Cavalry Troops. The cavalry Landwehr were mobilized into squadrons and attached to the Army Corps, and there were also reserve units of Artillery, etc.

Organization

The 25 Army Corps were the framework on which all German Army organization was based and served as the basis for all the wartime expansions. Each formed a complete, self-supporting entity and the Corps Commander was almost completely independent in his own area. He took orders directly from the Kaiser, or the King in Bavaria. He was responsible for the training of the troops under his command, although technical instruction of the various branches and services mainly rested with the various Inspectors General. He was allowed considerable latitude in regard to all matters of finance and administration within his own district, and it was this decentralization of both responsibility and command which was the fundamental reason why the German Army was able to mobilize so rapidly and which greatly facilitated its enormous expansion during the war years.

The peacetime strength of the Army in 1914 amounted in round numbers to 840,000 of all ranks but, by the end of 1917, this figure had risen to nearly 6,000,000, not including recruits under training at the time. An idea of the expansion can be gained from the increase in the 218 Active Infantry Regiments; 113 Reserve Regiments; 96 Landwehr Regiments, and miscellaneous battalions which, by 1918, had increased to 698 Active; 114 Reserve; and 106 Landwehr Regiments—this figure does not include the first and second term Landsturm. Some of the increases in the arms can be seen in the following table:

A medical officer wearing the 'Bluse'; the shoulder cords bear the Aesculapian Staff. (Courtesy G. A. Embleton)

It will be noted from these figures that the strength of the Cavalry remained almost stationary. The reason was that most of the cavalry units formed after the mobilization served solely as dismounted troops and are classified under infantry. By November 1918 the original 25 Army Corps had been expanded to include 24 Reserve Corps of which three were Bavarian, plus Landwehr, Landsturm, and even Naval Corps. In all, the Army Corps now totalled $218\frac{1}{2}$ divisions, three of which were stationed in Germany. They were made up as follows:

Unit	July 1914	Jan 1918
Infantry Battalions	669	2300
Cavalry Squadrons	550	570
Field Artillery Batteries	642	2900
Foot Artillery Batteries	400	2250
Pioneer Companies	150	650

Active and Independent Divisions	117
Reserve Divisions	$40\frac{1}{2}$
Landwehr Divisions	30
Ersatz Divisions	5
Bavarian Divisions	17
Alpine, Jäger and 3 Naval Divisions	6
Divisions:	$215\frac{1}{2}$
+ Divisions in Germany:	3
	$218\frac{1}{2}$

These divisions were deployed as follows:

Western Front (figure includes		
dismounted Cavalry Divisions)		$187\frac{1}{2}$
Eastern Front		20
Southern and Balkan Fronts		8
Germany		3
	Divisions:	$218\frac{1}{2}$

The contingents furnished by the various states to make up the confederated army in August 1914 were as follows:

Prussia and the smaller states	
including Brunswick, Baden,	
Oldenburg, Hesse etc.	78%
Bavaria	11%
Saxony	7%
Württemberg	4%

The strength of an average German Army Corps in August 1914 was as follows:

Two Infantry Divisions, each of two Brigades, each Brigade of two Infantry Regiments

One Foot Artillery Regiment of two Battalions each, each battalion having four batteries
One Field Artillery Brigade comprising two Field Artillery Regiments plus
Two Cavalry Brigades each comprising two Cavalry Regiments

Conscription and Mobilization

Due to the efficient system of conscription, Germany was able to field a large professional army within a few days of war being declared. In peacetime every German male, from his seventeenth to his forty-fifth birthday, was liable for some form of military service. Although not eligible for service with the Standing Army until his twentieth birthday, every man on reaching the age of seventeen became automatically liable to serve with the Landsturm (Home Guard).

A group of infantry in full marching order, 1914.

An early trench-raiding party of the 40th Fusilier Regiment. These were forerunners of the Assault Troops, Sturmbat-tailonen. The spikes have been removed from the tops of the helmets.

At twenty he commenced service with the Standing Army for a period of two years (three with the cavalry or artillery), followed by successive periods of seven years with the Reserve forces; the Landwehr for eleven years and then back to the Landsturm for a final seven years. After completing two or three years with the colours he was liable to be called for two annual trainings with the Reserve. This system of service was such that each year saw a constant entry from one form of military service to another until the forty-fifth year. Thus there was a considerable pool of manpower on the outbreak of hostilities. In wartime men could be called out and sent to the front before reaching their twentieth birthday and were not automatically released from further service on reaching forty-five. Furthermore, there was no transferring from one category

to another, from, say, the Landwehr to the Landsturm. Having served the requisite number of years of service a few men might be transferred, because of wounds or sickness.

In 1913 the annual contingent necessary to maintain the Army was approximately 305,000 men. As the annual call-up numbers were usually far in excess of this number, even after a thorough weeding out of the medically unfit, a certain number were transferred each year to the Ersatz (Supplementary) Reserve. This comprised men fit for active service who, because of economic or domestic reasons, were excused full military service; men with minor physical defects also came into this category. Normal service with the Ersatz Reserve was twelve years, during which time they were liable for call-up for three annual trainings. After the twelve years they passed into the second period Landsturm category. On mobilization in 1914 the Ersatz Reserve amounted to about 1,000,000 men aged between twenty and thirty-two years, and formed a high proportion of the Reserve Divisions.

There were two more important categories which formed the basis of the German Army. The first was the Restanten Liste, made up of men who were not taken for any form of service, but whose service was put back for one or more years, usually for special domestic or business reasons. After having been retarded for more than three successive musters, men were released from obligations to serve and were thereafter posted to Untrained Landsturm units. Second in this category was the Einjahrige Freiwilligen (One Year Volunteers). These were men of good education who undertook to clothe, equip and feed themselves during their period of service and who usually attained a high standard of proficiency in their duties. They were permitted to transfer to the Reserve as Offiziere Aspirant at the end of their one-year service; after undertaking two annual trainings with the Reserve and passing a military examination, they became Reserve Offiziere.

During the war a certain number of men between the ages of seventeen and twenty years were allowed to volunteer for active service before their official calling-up date; they were known as Kriegsfreiwilligen (War Volunteers).

The Reserve and Landwehr were practically all

absorbed by expansions of the Army in 1914; the Landsturm, in particular, was extensively drawn upon to make up for the losses of the winter campaigns of 1914. By the end of 1915 the second category Zweite Ban was practically exhausted. As a result, normal categories gradually found themselves called earlier until, by 1917, classes who would not normally have expected to have been called to the colours until 1919, were being drafted for service on the Russian and Balkan Fronts to enable more seasoned and experienced men to move to the Western Front to replace the enormous losses being endured there.

The German recruiting system was based on the territorial division of the Empire, 25 Army Corps being the unit for all purposes of recruitment and administration. Germany was divided into 24 Army Corps Districts in each of which a complete Army Corps was stationed and recruited. In addition the Prussian Guard Corps, excluded from the numbered sequence, was raised from the whole of Prussia and Alsace-Lorraine but, because of its Guard functions, was stationed in Berlin.

In time of peace each of the Army Corps Districts was divided into four or five Brigade Districts, each in turn divided into two or three Landwehr Districts.

The Army Corps Districts were as follows:

Army Corps	District	Headquarters
Guard	Prussia and Alsace-Lorraine	Berlin
I	East Prussia	Königsberg
II	Pommerania	Stettin
III	Brandenburg	Berlin

The crew of an '08 machine gun, 1914. Note the dragging harness on three of the crew.

Army Corps	District	Headquarters	Army Corps	District	Headquarters
IV	Prussian Saxony	Magdeburg	XVIII	Hesse	Frankfurt a/M
V	Duchy of Posen	Posen	XIX	Western Saxony	Leipzig
VI	Silesia	Breslau	XX	South East Prussia	Allenstein
VII	Westphalia	Munster	XXI	Eastern Lorraine	Saarbrücken
VIII	Rhineland	Coblenz			
IX	Schleswig-Holstein	Altona	I Bavarian	Southern Bavaria	Munich
X	Hanover	Hanover	II Bavarian	Lower Franconia and Palatinate	Wurzburg
XI	Thuringia and Hesse-Nassau	Cassel	III Bavarian	Northern Bavaria	Nuremberg
XII	Eastern Saxony	Dresden			
XIII	Württemberg	Stuttgart			
XIV	Baden	Karlsruhe			
XV	Alsace	Strasbourg			
XVI	Western Lorraine	Metz			
XVII	West Prussia	Danzig			

A machine-gun Scharfschützen Kompagnie, photographed in 1915. Their special badge is on the left upper sleeve. The coloured cap bands are covered by field-grey strips which also cover the state cockades. The man on the extreme left has modified round cuffs on his tunic. The gun has a telescopic sight.

THE ARTILLERY

This was the elite arm of the German Army. It comprised Field (including Horse Artillery) and Foot Artillery, which had under its jurisdiction all the heavy pieces including howitzers and mortars, and during the course of the war, Mountain

A group of Pioneers of the 8th Pioneer Battalion, mid-1916; the photograph shows both the modified 1910 jacket and the 'Bluse' being worn. The caps have black bands and some of the men wear black shoulder straps.

Artillery which had no peacetime establishment and was formed as part of the Foot Artillery. (In this short work it is impossible to list every pattern and type of artillery used by the German Army during the war, as a great many foreign and captured guns were used besides the sixty-seven or more standard guns, but some of the extensively used pieces are given.) Prior to the outbreak of war there were 642 batteries of Field and Horse Artillery, this figure being increased to about 2,900 batteries by 1918.

THE FIELD ARTILLERY

This was normally equipped with one of three types of 10·5cm light field howitzer and permanently attached to an infantry division. The Horse Batteries were attached to Cavalry Divisions and were equipped with one of five types of 7·7cm field gun.

In peacetime batteries consisted of six field guns, or four light field howitzers. By 1915 all Field Batteries were reduced to four guns in order to provide material for new formations. During 1916 a series of Independent Field Artillery Batteries numbered 801–915 were formed. These batteries were used to reinforce the divisional artillery on the Eastern Front.

During the early stages of the war Divisional Artillery organization varied in the Active, Reserve and newer formations, but in general were as follows: in each Artillery Brigade were two Field Artillery Regiments each of two Abteilungen, comprising three or four batteries each. The Abteilungen were numbered I and II, and the Batteries in Arabic numerals from 1 to 6 in each regiment. The newly formed formations raised after mobilization differed. The Batteries were reduced from 12 to 9. These 9 formed one Field Artillery Regiment and were divided into three Abteilungen, two of which were now armed with field guns and a third with light field howitzers. By 1918 Field Howitzer Batteries formed one third of the total Field Artillery. Before the war light field howitzers comprised one-eighth of the total as only one Abteilung in each Army Corps was armed with the piece. A Field Battery was commanded by a Captain and organized in two sections (Zuge) each commanded by a junior officer. A third subaltern acted as supervisor to the ammunition supply, in

Left:
Pioneer of a Field Company of the 14th Pioneer Battalion in full marching order, 1914. Note the unit designation on the front of the helmet cover and the 'Swedish' pattern of cuff.

Right:
Two members of a Field Artillery unit. The man on the right is a gunner, and the one on the left is a driver. The gunner is armed with a rifle, although normally he would be armed with a carbine. The driver is armed with the Reichs M79 revolver and a sword; he wears the cavalry-pattern open-buckled waistbelt. Note the ball mount on top of the 'pickelhaube'.

some cases there was a fourth who acted as a forward observation officer and in some, a fifth attached to transport duties.

THE FOOT ARTILLERY

Prior to the outbreak of war, Foot Artillery comprised 24 Regiments, one for each Army Corps district. Each Foot Artillery Regiment was divided into two battalions of four batteries each. Arma-ment comprised one of four types of 15cm heavy field howitzer and 21cm mortars (heavy howitzers). The battalion equipped with the mortars had only two batteries. The peacetime establishment for heavy Artillery was 400 batteries, but by the end of the war this had been expanded to 2,250 batteries. Each of the Active Foot Artillery Regiments had its complementary Reserve Regiment, and as production of heavy guns increased Landwehr, Landsturm and Ersatz Depot Battalions were also mobilized. The number of battalions in a Regiment were also increased, some having as many as five. In addition, a number of independent batteries were formed and numbered from 101 to 150 and from 200 to 800. Many of these batteries were armed with captured pieces.

The organization and command of Foot Batteries was complex but in general the allocation of heavy guns was as follows: Batteries were allotted to certain sectors of the front in accordance with tactical objectives, or the situation of a particular sector of the front at a given time. The normal allotment for a quiet sector was eight or nine batteries for each divisional sector, but 16 batteries were normally allocated to a battle front.

The very heavy calibre pieces and long-range weapons were normally on railway mountings and grouped together for counter battery work or for special tasks under higher command. Other batteries were under orders of the Divisional Artillery Commander in whose sector they were placed. When the Division moved the Batteries generally stayed where they were. In active battle sectors a Corps was often given a special HQ Artillery Staff which kept in touch with various artillery staff within the Corps and directly controlled Corps long-range heavy-artillery groups. The Head-quarters of every Army was provided with an Artillery Adviser of General Officer rank.

The organization of Foot Artillery Batteries varied according to calibre of the pieces. The normal number of guns in Foot Artillery Batteries was as follows:

Nature of the battery	Number of guns or howitzers
10cm guns	4
13cm guns	2
15cm guns	2
15cm howitzers	4
21cm mortars	3
24cm naval guns (mounted on wheeled carriages, on railway mountings or on platform mountings)	—

Note that in the German Artillery the term 'mortar' did not allude to trench mortars, but to any howitzer of 21cm upwards.

MOUNTAIN ARTILLERY

During the course of the war about 25 Mountain Batteries were formed and grouped in Abteilungen of three batteries each. They were allotted to divisions fighting in the Balkans, Carpathian Mountains, Alps and in the Vosges. The personnel serving these batteries were mainly drawn from Bavaria, Württemberg and Baden.

A Mountain Battery comprised four 7·5cm quick-firing mountain guns organized for mule pack transport, the complete gun forming seven loads. A few batteries were armed with mountain howitzers. The establishment of a section of a mountain battery were 2 junior officers, 1 sergeant major, 6 corporals, 1 mounted orderly, 26 gunners, 31 drivers, 2 train drivers, 2 mountain guns, 31 mules and 10 riding horses.

ARTILLERY UNIT STRENGTHS

(excluding the elaborate transport and ammunition waggon strength)

Field Artillery Mobile Battery
5 officers, 148 other ranks, 139 horses, 6 guns, 6 munition waggons. The Battery was sometimes broken down into 3 sections of 2 guns each.

Generalmajor v. Uechtritz und Steinkirch, commander of the 41st Cavalry Brigade, 1914/17. He is dressed in the field-grey uniform of the Hussars. The regimental distinction of the 17th Brunswick Hussars is worn between the cockades on the cap.

A cavalry trooper of the 1st Saxon Reiter Regiment in field-service dress. (Courtesy R. G. Harris Collection)

Horse Artillery Battery
4 officers, 133 other ranks, 180 horses, 4 guns and 4 ammunition waggons.

Horse Artillery Battalion
3 batteries of 4 guns each, 20 officers, 429 other ranks and 578 horses. The staff comprised 8 officers, 30 other ranks and 38 horses. Each battalion was attached to a cavalry division.

Field Artillery Regiment
2 battalions of 3 batteries each, plus a light ammunition column. 2 regiments formed a brigade which was attached to an infantry division. Commanded by a major general.

Heavy Artillery
Heavy artillery regiments were primarily used for garrison and coastal defence and for siege operations against fortified positions. Their main armaments were the howitzer, heavy mortar and siege gun.

Heavy artillery was organized into 2 battalions of 4 batteries each.

Howitzer Battery
6 officers, 224 other ranks, 148 horses and 4 munition waggons.

Heavy Mortar Battery
6 officers, 249 other ranks, 148 horses and 4 munition waggons.

Field Howitzer Battalion
4 batteries and 1 ammunition column. 37 officers, 1,178 other ranks, 707 horses. Staff comprised 8 officers and 21 other ranks.

Heavy Mortar Battalion
Two batteries and an ammunition column. 25 officers and 780 other ranks, 515 horses. The same staff as the Field Howitzer Battalion.

Park or Depot Companies
of Foot Artillery Batteries comprised 5 officers, 248 other ranks and 10 horses.

Ammunition Columns and Train
Included various supply, transportation and support units all combined and organized as a Train Battalion. It was responsible for transporting ammunition, food, forage and other necessaries. Each of the Battalions supported an Army Corps in the field. Additional responsibilities included remount detachments, medical companies, field bakeries, etc. The Staff of the Train Battalion comprised 3 officers and 11 other ranks with 12 horses.

THE INFANTRY

German infantry were organized in Regiments, each of three battalions numbered I, II and III. Each Battalion consisted of four companies, plus a machine-gun company. The Companies were numbered 1 to 12 throughout the regiment and the machine-gun companies were numbered 1, 2 and 3. The company was split into three Platoons numbered 1, 2 and 3 within each company. Each Platoon was in turn divided into four sections numbered throughout the company 1 to 12. The smallest sub-division was the Squad comprising eight men and a lance-corporal. Each company had four stretcher-bearers.

The Regiment was commanded by a colonel with a lieutenant-colonel (Oberstleutnant) as second-in-command; however, during the war it was not unusual to find a regiment commanded by a major. Each Battalion was commanded by a major and each Company by a captain or, in some cases, a lieutenant. A Section was commanded by a corporal, and the Squad by a lance-corporal.

A Prussian War Ministry Order dated 12 March 1917 reduced the strength of a battalion to 750 other ranks. This reduction was necessitated by the introduction of three light machine guns ('08/15' pattern) to each company. At the end of 1917 it was estimated that a battalion had a strength of 800 other ranks. In 1918 this figure was increased to 850 excluding the machine guns. Without the machine-gun companies the war establishment of Infantry was as follows:

Battalion: 23 officers including supply officer; 3 medical officers and paymasters; 1,050 other ranks; 59 horses; 19 waggons

Regiment: 73 officers; 10 medical officers and paymasters; 3,204 other ranks; 93 horses; 59 waggons. The Staff comprised 4 officers; including a transport officer, 1 medical officer and paymaster; 54 other ranks; 16 horses and 2 waggons

Company: 5 officers; 259 other ranks; 10 horses and 4 waggons

As the war progressed, some Independent Battalions were combined into new regiments, but specialist 'Jäger', 'Schützen', ski and mountain units still maintained their independent status. The Jäger Battalions, one of which was attached to each Army Corps, comprised specially selected men from forest areas who wore distinctive uniforms. In 1916 most of the Jäger Battalions were formed into regiments, and in 1917 a Jäger Division was formed to take part in the Italian Campaign.

During 1915 and 1916 trench warfare demanded specialist companies, detachments and sections to be attached to the infantry regiments. Artificers—men with special trade qualifications—were selected from battalions, formed into Regimental Pioneer Companies, Entrenching and Tunnelling Companies, and Concrete Construction Companies.

As the formation of these specialist units reduced the strength of the rifle companies, the practice was finally discouraged and special regular units were formed to carry out these duties. The experience of 1916 led the Germans to organize within each infantry unit three types of special troops:

Machine-Gun Sections, 2 per company each armed with three 08/15 Light Machine Guns

Trench Mortar Detachments, 1 to a battalion each armed with 4 light mortars

Signalling Detachments, of varying strengths.

The men forming these units were not supernumary to regimental establishment, but remained on the nominal rolls of the companies from which they were drawn. Prior to mobilization, only the Jäger Battalions had cyclists each having one or two companies mounted in that fashion. During the war additional cyclist companies were formed, and by 1917 there were about 150 of these. Later a number of the companies were formed into battalions and finally three were formed into a

Two members of the 11th (2nd Westphalian) Hussars in field-grey service dress.

Three members of an infantry unit dressed for the trenches. They wear waterproof overtrousers and carry extra ammunition in cotton bandoliers. The ammunition pouches worn by the man on the left are of an obsolete pattern; when they were laden with cartridges they had to be supported by an additional strap worn halter-fashion around the neck.

cyclist brigade which, in March 1917, did good work covering the retreat to the Hindenburg Line. Other cyclist troops guarded the Belgian/Dutch border.

In peacetime a few Jäger Battalions were trained annually in mountain and winter warfare. During the war these men formed the cadres of four ski battalions raised in Bavaria and one battalion in Württemberg. The 1st, 2nd and 3rd Ski Battalions formed the 3rd Jäger Regiment in the Alpine Corps. These Battalions, brought into being in the spring of 1915, were sent to Trentino. Afterwards they served in Serbia, and in the spring of 1916 were transferred to the Western Front where they took part in the Battle for Verdun. In August 1916 they were sent to the Carpathians and were attached to the 200th Division.

The Württemberg Ski Battalion fought in the Vosges Mountains until 1st October 1916, then transferred to Transylvania. In the spring of 1917 it returned to the Vosges and later went to the Italian front.

The war establishment transport of an Infantry Regiment of three battalions, exclusive of the machine-gun companies, consisted of 16 led horses, 58 two-horsed waggons and one four-horse waggon. It was organized with 16 led horses as first-line transport, together with 12 small arm ammunition waggons and 12 travelling kitchens. The baggage consisted of 16 baggage waggons, 122 supply waggons, 3 sutler waggons and a tool waggon. The transport was all four-horsed, painted grey. The first line transport of a Battalion without the machine-gun company included 4 led horses, 4 small arms ammunition waggons, 4 travelling kitchens and an infantry medical store waggon. The Train for Battalion HQ consisted of 4 company baggage waggons and 5 supply waggons including 1 sutlers waggon. The transport of a Company included 1 led horse, 1 company small arms ammunition waggon carrying 14,000 rounds, 1 travelling kitchen, 1 company baggage waggon and a company supply waggon.

ASSAULT DETACHMENTS

The Germans were quick to realize the potential of developing elite detachments of specially picked men to act as assault parties and trench raiding detachments. The men were handpicked for courage and initiative and were trained in special techniques necessary to fight in the narrow and dangerous confines of the trench systems.

Assault Companies were first used at Verdun and originally comprised three-man teams. The technique involved attacking the trench in flank, the first of the trio armed with a shield made from a machine-gun shield mounting and a sharpened entrenching tool, followed by the second man carrying haversacks full of short-fused stick grenades, and the third would follow up armed with a knife or bayonet. The Stosstruppe proved so successful that the system was further developed until, in 1916, Sturmkompanie were formed and attached to divisions on a permanent basis. These Assault Companies comprised an officer and 120 other ranks, and were organized in three platoons, one of which was attached to each regiment in the division. By 1918 most armies on the Western Front had expanded units known as Sturmbataillone comprising 4 assault companies, an infantry gun battery armed with a 3·7cm piece, a light trench mortar detachment, a flame thrower detachment, a machine-gun company and an HQ sometimes called Park Company. When not in action the men served as instructors training new recruits for the units.

The following Sturmbataillone and Sturmkompanie are known to have existed in 1918:

Battalion	Army to which the unit was attached	Battalion	Army to which the unit was attached
1st (company)	1st	11th	19th
2nd	3rd	12th (company)	7th
3rd	7th	13th	East
4th (company)	4th	14th	Army C
5th Rohr*	5th	15th Bavarian	Army A
6th Bavarian	6th	16th	Army B
7th	7th	17th (company)	4th
8th	17th	18th (company)	18th
10th	Eastern Front		

*This was named after Hauptmann Ulrich Rohr who was the man mainly responsible for the original idea of these highly successful formations. He personally designed much of the technical equipment which they used in action.

THE CAVALRY

In peacetime German cavalry was not organized in Divisions, except for the Guard. Each Army Corps District had two or three cavalry brigades. At the outbreak of war eleven Cavalry Divisions were formed. Regiments surplus to the requirements of the Divisions became the Divisional Cavalry of Infantry Divisions. A few Cavalry Brigades worked independently.

At the outbreak of war German cavalry comprised 110 Regiments* each of five squadrons. On mobilization each regiment moved off leaving one squadron at its home station to act as the Depot Squadron.

The war establishment of the Squadron was 4 officers, 163 other ranks, 178 horses and three

* Kürassiers, Dragoons, Lancers, Hussars, Heavy Cavalry, Light Cavalry and Mounted Rifles.

A group belonging to one of the Guard Grenadier Regiments, 1916. They are all wearing the newly introduced steel trench helmet, but only the centre figure in the rear is wearing the 'Bluse'. Note the figure in the front wearing puttees.

waggons. Eleven Cavalry Divisions were formed on mobilization, each of three cavalry brigades. Each Brigade comprised two regiments. Each Regiment had four squadrons, plus a Machine-Gun Squadron and the Depot Squadron. To each Cavalry Division was attached 1 Jäger Battalion, three Batteries of Horse Artillery, one or two Cyclist Companies, a Machine-Gun Detachment, a Cavalry Pioneer Detachment, comprising 1 officer and 33 other ranks, and a Signals Detachment. The war establishment of a Cavalry Division was 283 officers, 4,995 other ranks, 5,590 horses and 216 waggons.

In 1914 the two or three squadrons of cavalry attached to each Infantry Division were known as Divisional Cavalry. Later in the war a single squadron only was allotted to each Infantry Division. During the period of intense trench warfare squadrons of dismounted cavalry assisted the infantry by taking their turn in the trenches. When not thus engaged these dismounted troopers patrolled roads, acted as prisoner escorts, and took their turn in picket and outpost duties as well as mounting-up as orderlies.

Thirty-nine Reserve Cavalry Regiments were formed during the war together with a number of

A group of the 2nd Squadron of the 1st Saxon Reiter Regiment, December 1914. Note the spurs on the boots, also the rank distinctions of the senior NCO in the centre. (R. G. Harris Collection)

Ersatz, Landwehr and Landsturm Squadrons, but the latter were mainly used to patrol frontiers and to guard lines of communication.

During the period 1916–17 a number of regiments employed as Divisional Cavalry were withdrawn from the front, dismounted and converted into Cavalry/Rifle Regiments, most being of the Reserve or Ersatz formations. These dismounted cavalry rifle regiments were equivalent to infantry battalions and were organized as four squadrons plus a Machine-Gun Company. Each squadron comprised three troops and a trench mortar detachment resembling an infantry company. The units were attached to infantry divisions and were normally allocated quiet parts of the front, allowing more experienced troops to be utilized elsewhere. By the end of 1917 about 50 of these regiments had been dismounted.

MACHINE-GUN UNITS

The German High Command was quick to appreciate the strategical importance of the machine gun prior to the outbreak of the war, and this awareness, plus the ever-increasing success of the weapon in subsequent static trench warfare conditions, was a prime factor in deciding the outcome of so many of the Western Front battles.

In 1914 every Infantry Regiment and Jäger

Battalion had a Machine-Gun Company with an establishment of 6 guns and 1 spare. In addition there were a number of independent field and fortress machine-gun detachments which, during the early stages of the conflict, were rapidly absorbed to provide machine guns for newly raised formations. As the demand for machine guns grew, and the output increased, a number of new sections were formed. These supplementary sections consisted of an officer and 30–40 men armed with three or four machine guns. One or two were attached to Infantry Regiments as required and, in some cases, they were absorbed to form a second machine-gun company for the regiment to which they were attached. By the end of 1915 several regiments possessed two machine-gun companies in this way. During the winter of 1915–16 a new type of machine-gun unit was formed and trained for the purpose of developing the power of the arm. These units, known as Machine-Gun Marksman Sections, were formed from picked gunners who underwent a special four- or five-week course

Left:
A rifleman of the 10th Jäger Battalion, 1915. He wears puttees and mountain boots and carries a special mountaineering rucksack in place of the normal calfskin knapsack. All leather equipment is natural colour. The shako cover appears to have a piping around the upper edge which would have been green, as would the piping on the collar, cuffs and front of the tunic. (R. G. Harris Collection)

Centre:
A member of Mountain Artillery Battery No. 2, 1914/15. He wears puttees, mountain boots, and carries the long artillery pattern '08 pistol with detachable butt (carried on the back of the holster). Extra magazines are carried on the waistbelt. (R. G. Harris Collection)

Right:
An infantryman in 1917 wearing full trench body armour. Worn mainly by snipers, some machine gunners in exposed positions, and members of some assault units, its weight made it unpopular. (R. Marrion Collection)

especially directed towards the use of the machine gun in attack.

The elite units began to arrive on the Western Front early in 1916 and were first employed at Verdun in March of that year. They were allotted to Infantry Regiments engaged in offensive operations, or holding particularly difficult sectors. The total number of Marksman Sections formed was

21

about 200, i.e. roughly one to a Division. Their establishment was 1 captain or lieutenant, 1 sergeant major, 6 corporals (gun commanders), 20 lance-corporals, 40 gunners, 1 cyclist orderly, 1 armourer, 1 medical corporal—a total of 1 officer and 78 other ranks.

By the beginning of 1916 the number of machine guns had increased from 1,600 to something over 8,000. As a result a separate Inspectorate became necessary. By July of that year the number of machine guns had increased to 11,000 (this number included many captured weapons), but there was still no standard organization, and the successive creation of various loosely formed units led to an irregular allotment of weapons to infantry formations. In some cases regiments had 6, while others boasted as many as 25 machine guns. The situation was standardized in August 1916, when regular machine gun units were raised and the machine company of six guns was adopted as the standard formation. A Staff Officer for Machine Guns was added to the HQ of each Army Corps and by the end of 1916 the number of machine guns in use had increased to 16,000.

Regimental Machine-Gun Companies. Every Infantry Regiment had three companies numbered 1 to 3.

A Kürassier patrol in Eastern Europe at the outbreak of the war.

One company was attached to each battalion, and at Regimental HQ was the Regimental Machine Gun Officer, who was responsible for the supervision of all three companies. The 2nd and 3rd machine gun companies in each regiment were formed by absorbing existing Sections and Detachments attached to the regiment.

Machine-Gun Marksman Sections. These were converted into companies with an establishment identical to the Regimental Companies. However, they were not attached to Infantry Regiments but combined in groups of three or four to form Detachments which acted as a reserve at the disposal of GHQ. One Detachment was normally attached to a Division actively engaged in the line and, as elite units, they wore on the left upper sleeve a special badge representing the machine gun. By 1917 there was a further increase in the requirement of the machine gun and this involved a reorganization. The greatest change was in the number of guns allocated to each company. This was gradually increased to 12 guns, and the various types of machine gun in use were superseded by the M '08/15 pattern which were issued to all infantry battalions. By the end of 1917 every infantry company on the Western Front had received three of these new light machine guns and some companies were equipped with six. By the beginning

of 1918 each Division on the Western Front in an active sector had on average 108 light and 144 M '08 machine guns.

The establishment of the Machine Gun Company was 4 officers, 133 other ranks, 2 riding horses, 18 draught horses and 9 two-horsed waggons. There were also 6 hand carts for the '08 guns drawn by 2 men.

SPECIAL MACHINE-GUN UNITS

Fifty Mountain Machine-Gun Detachments were formed and specially equipped for Alpine warfare. They were at one time employed in the Vosges but later transferred to the Carpathians and the Balkan theatre. The personnel wore the uniform of the mountain troops.

Machine-Gun Companies of the Cyclist Battalions. Formed in 1916, they were extensively used in the Rumanian campaign. The companies were organized in three troops of two guns. The machine guns were mounted on motor lorries and each troop was transported by lorry with guns and ammunition enabling each to act as an independent unit. The lorry carried 15,000 rounds of ammunition. The establishment was 3 officers, 46 other ranks, plus one motor cyclist, 12 lorry drivers and three Train soldiers. Transport was two 3-ton lorries (one for baggage and tools etc.), and a four-horse waggon for supplies. The companies were armed with pistols and all NCOs carried binoculars.

Cavalry Machine-Gun Units. Before 1914 there were no machine-gun units attached to cavalry formations. There were, however, eleven independent Machine-Gun Batteries which, on mobilization, were allotted to the eleven cavalry divisions. A Jäger Battalion, together with its machine-gun company, was also attached to each cavalry division. During 1916 a Machine-Gun Section was attached to each cavalry regiment, and these were finally expanded into Machine-Gun Squadrons, each armed with 6 guns.

Anti-Aircraft Machine-Gun Detachments. During 1917 two series of these units were formed. The first was numbered from 801 upwards, the second from 901

An assault detachment wearing full body armour. (R. Marrion Collection)

upwards. Known as 'Flamga', each detachment consisted of about 80 men under the command of a lieutenant or a captain. They were issued with 12 machine guns of the M '08 pattern, each gun served by an NCO and 5 men.

Light Machine-Gun Sections. Formed in 1916, these sections had an establishment of 1 officer and 44 other ranks and were armed with the Bergmann L.M.G. 15. This weapon, sometimes referred to as the Bergmann automatic rifle, was manufactured at Suhl and had the same barrel as the M '08 weapon with a similar range, but was only sighted up to 400 metres and was intended for close-range use. About 111 of these sections were raised.

Musketen Battalions. Three battalions each 500 strong were formed in 1915. Split into sections of four men armed with one automatic rifle, they were used as reserve formations stationed to the rear of front-line trenches; their function was to halt any breakthrough that might occur in a particular sector. They proved successful at this task, but in 1916 one battalion was disbanded and the personnel used to bolster other machine-gun units.

ENGINEERS AND PIONEERS

There were three corps of the German Army whose duties roughly corresponded with those of our own Royal Engineers: the Corps of Engineers, the Fortress Construction Officers and the Corps of Pioneers. All three corps came under the control of the Inspector General of the Engineer Pioneer Corps and there was a General Officer of the Inspectorate attached to each General Headquarters on the Western Front.

The Corps of Engineers and the Fortress Construction Officers. The Corps was concerned solely with the design, construction, maintenance and organization of fortresses, and consisted only of officers. Engineer Officers received the same training as their fellow officers in the Pioneer Corps and were interchangeable. *The Fortress Construction Officers* were commissioned from qualified senior NCOs of the Pioneer Corps after receiving special training.

The Pioneer Corps carried out all the works connected with field engineering, and comprised the following elements: Field Companies, Mining Companies, Bridging Trains, Searchlight Sections, Park Companies. The Pioneers also furnished troops for the *Trench-Mortar Units, Flame-Throwing Units,* and for operating poison-gas apparatus. A number of electrical technicians were formed into units responsible for running power supplies to the front line. There was one *Pioneer Battalion* of four companies attached to each Army Corps and 8 Battalions of Fortress Engineers on the peacetime establishment. By May 1917 the Pioneer units in each Division were re-organized and re-grouped into *Pioneer Battalions.* A Divisional Pioneer Battalion comprised 2 Field Companies, a Trench-Mortar Company and a Searchlight Section.

Pioneer Regiments. The 8 original Fortress Battalions were expanded at the outbreak of war into 10 Pioneer Regiments. Each regiment comprised 4–6 Field Companies, plus a Park Company and several Reserve and Ersatz Companies. By the end of 1917 there were nearly 700 companies available to Divisions enabling 2 companies or more to be on the Divisional strength, instead of the three for each Army Corps on mobilization.

The establishment of a Pioneer Field Company was 4 officers; 1 medical officer; 1 paymaster; 262 other ranks; 26 horses; 7 waggons. The company was organized in three sections which could act independently. No bridging equipment was carried.

Mining Companies. Before 1914 mining was carried out by the Fortress Battalions. When trench warfare broke out, mining became more important and was undertaken by companies of the Pioneer Regiments. They were gradually supplemented by trained miners taken from infantry units and formed into units which were improvised under regimental arrangements. It was not until 1916 that a regular series of mining companies were formed, but by 1918 there were over 50 such units. The establishment was 4 officers and 250 other ranks on an active part of the front.

Bridging Trains. These were formally attached to Divisions, Army Corps or Armies, but at the end of 1916 they were withdrawn from the lower formations and attached thereafter to the Armies as required. The establishment was 2 officers, 59 other ranks, 98 horses, 21 waggons, 12 pontoon waggons with all the bridging materials each carrying half a pontoon, 2 trestle waggons, 1 shore transom waggon, all pulled by four horse teams. The personnel of the waggons were all drawn from the Train.

THE AIR SERVICE

In 1914 there were five Airship Battalions of three and four companies. The 2nd company of the 3rd Battalion was Saxon and the 4th company of the 4th Battalion a Württemberg detachment. In addition there were four Aircraft Battalions (*Flieger Bataillone*) and a Bavarian Flieger Bataillone. The 1st Battalion, stationed at Doberitz, was a Saxon formation; the 2nd was at Posen, the third at Cologne, and the 4th at Strasbourg, each with companies at outlying towns. Before mobilization they were considered part of the Communication Troops, but in 1916 were established as the Air Forces (Luftstreitkräfte) as a separate branch of the Army, taking precedence over the Pioneers and Communication Branches.

1 Trooper, 3rd Brandenburg Hussar Rgt., 1914
2 Grenadier, 1st Prussian Guard 'Kaiser Alexander Grenadier Rgt.', 1914
3 2nd Lieutenant, 1st Prussian Foot Guards, 1914
4 Trooper, 2nd Prussian Guard Machine Gun Detachment, 1914

G. A. EMBLETON

A

1 Trooper, 3rd Kürassier Rgt., 1914
2 Trooper, 5th Westphalian Ulan Rgt., 1914
3 Trooper, 6th Magdeburg Dragoon Rgt., 1914

B

G.A. EMBLETON

1 & 3 Privates, 76th (2nd Hanseatic) Hamburg Inf. Rgt., 1915
2 Private, 7th Coy., 2nd Bn. of a Prussian Inf. Rgt., 1915
4 Jäger, 9th Lauernberg Jäger Bn., 1915
5 Private, 55th (6th Westphalian) Inf. Rgt., 1915
6 Private, 8th Coy., 2nd Bn., 102nd Royal Saxon Inf. Rgt., 1915

G. A. EMBLETON

C

1 **Landsturmann, 12th Ellwagen (Westphalian) Landsturm Bn., 1915**
2 **Captain, 9th Bn., Prussian Train, 1915**
3 **Captain, Prussian General Staff, 1915**
4 **General Officer, 1915**

D

1 2nd Lieutenant, 13th Foot Artillery Rgt., 1916
2 Gefreite, 110th Baden Reserve Grenadier Rgt., 1916
3 Unteroffizier, 63rd (4th Silesian) Inf. Rgt., 1916
4 Gunner, 2nd Troop, 5th Battery, 21st Field
   Artillery Rgt., 1916
5 NCO Specialist, Prussian Guard Reserve
   Pioneer Rgt., 1916

G. A. EMBLETON

E

1 Private, infantry, Palestine, 1916
2 Private, artillery, Palestine, 1916
3 Private, 1st Masurian Inf. Rgt., Palestine, 1916
4 Trooper, 6th Thuringian Ulan Rgt., Macedonia, 1917
5 Trooper, mountain machine gun battery, Macedonia, 1917
6 Jäger, Prussian Guard Bn., Macedonia, 1917

F

G. A. EMBLETON

1 2nd Lieutenant, Württemberg Ski Coy., 1917
2 2nd Lieutenant, Württemberg Mountain Bn., 1917
3 2nd Lieutenant, Prussian Guard-Schützen Bn.,
   walking-out dress, 1916-17

G. A. EMBLETON

G

Assault troops, 1917-18

1 NCO, Bavarian assault battalion
2 NCO, 5th Stürmbataillon 'Rohr'
3 Assault infantryman
4 Private, Assault Coy., 23rd Saxon
  (1st Saxon) Reserve Division

G. A. EMBLETON

Aeroplane and Observation. Balloon units were allotted to Armies as situations required and each Army in the field was provided with an *Army Aircraft Park* receiving new machines as they arrived from the factory. Pools of personnel were also maintained which were drafted to units in the field as the need arose. The standard aviation unit was a flight of about 115–120 all ranks.*

THE SIGNALS SERVICE

Before mobilization the personnel of the Signal Service was provided by the Telegraph troops and consisted of 6 Prussian Telegraph Battalions, 7 Fortress Telephone Companies, 1 Saxon Telegraph Battalion and 1 Fortress Telephone Company, 1 Württemberg Telegraph Company and 1 Fortress Telephone Detachment and 2 Bavarian Telegraph Battalions. Officers were mainly drawn from the Engineering and Pioneer branches, but some were from Infantry and Railway units. In January 1917 Telegraph troops were separated from Communication troops and organized as a separate Corps.

TRANSPORT AND COMMUNICATION SERVICES

Communication Troops were formerly responsible for Railway and Mechanical Transport Services but, when the Air Service and Signals Corps were separated, all Transportation units, when in the field, were put under the command of the Quartermaster-General's Department. The Service was divided into two branches: *The Railway Service* and the *Mechanical Transport Service.*

A peacetime establishment of railway personnel comprised: 3 Prussian Railway Regiments of eight companies each; 1 Prussian Railway Battalion of 4 companies; 1 Bavarian Railway Battalion of 3 companies; 3 Railway Traffic Companies.

Troop movements were the responsibility of an Army Railway Representative attached to each Army Corps line of communication area. He was also responsible for all repairs to tracks and to canal systems.

*For details of the evolution of this branch after the outbreak of war, see 'German Fighter Units 1914–17', by Alex Imrie, title No. 13 in the Osprey Airwar Series.

During the course of the war personnel were reorganized as follows: Railway Construction Companies; Rail Traffic Companies; 5 Railway Work Battalions; 9 Supplementary Battalions; 23 Railway Store Companies.

There were at least 13 Armoured Trains operating on the Western Front. Each Railway Construction and Traffic Company was affiliated to the depot of the Railway Regiment from which it was formed and wore that number below an 'E' on their shoulder straps.

Like the railway troops, mechanical transport became a separate entity in the December 1916 reorganization, and thereafter had its own Inspectorate. The *Director of Mechanical Transport* normally held the rank of a brigade commander and was under the direct orders from Quartermaster General's Department.

At the Headquarters of each Army in the Field was a *Commander of Mechanical Transport* who held the rank of a battalion commander. He had a staff of 5 officers and 27 other ranks. Each army had a *Mechanical Transport Park*, maintaining a pool of staff cars and lorries, a motor-cycle detachment, a postal lorry park, a motor ambulance convoy and a tractor park for the artillery.

Also attached to each Army were a varying number of lorry columns. Early in the war mechanical transport columns were allocated to Army Corps, but in 1916 they were sub-divided and converted into divisional units.

A Divisional Mechanical Transport Column comprised from 6 to 12 lorries and was allotted permanently to each division. The units were numbered in series as follows:

Nos.
500 upwards, to units in Palestine and Syria
530 upwards, Prussian, Saxon, Württemberg
    Active Divs
680 upwards, Bavarian Active Divs
700 upwards, Prussian, Saxon, Württemberg
    Reserve Divs
750 upwards, Bavarian Reserve Divs
760 upwards, Ersatz Divs
770 upwards, Landwehr Divs

As the war progressed and the securing of supplies became more difficult, the use of mechanical transport became more restricted and was utilized only when rail services became overtaxed or unavailable.

MEDICAL SERVICES

The German Army Medical Service consisted of a corps of officers designated Militär-Ärzte (Military Doctors), with ranks ranging from General-Stabs-Ärzte to Assistent Ärzte and Einjährige Ärzte. The rank and file were known as Santitäts-Mannschaften (Medical Service Troops) and included hospital orderlies and stretcher-bearers.

The Medical Service in the Field comprised a Regimental Medical Service; Bearer Companies (Field Ambulance units); Field Hospitals; Motor Ambulance Columns; War Hospitals; Ambulance Trains and Advanced Depots of Army Medical Stores. Normally there were two medical officers to each Battalion and 4 medical NCOs (a fifth was added after May 1916). The stretcher-bearers were considered non-combatants and were distinguished by a white brassard with a red cross on it, worn on the left upper sleeve of the tunic.

VETERINARY SERVICES

It was essential that an army which relied so much on horses for transportation purposes, and with such a large cavalry force, had an efficient veterinary branch.

The Veterinary Services were re-organized in 1910, and a new range of titles given to the officers were as follows: *General-Veterinär* (Colonel); *Korps-Stabs-Veterinär* (Lieutenant-Colonel or Major); *Ober-Stabs-Veterinär* (Major); *Stabs-Veterinär* ('Rittmeister'—Captain); *Ober-Veterinär* (1st Lieutenant); *Veterinär* (2nd Lieutenant). The corps was under the command of a *Director-General of Veterinary Services* who had three Assistant Directors in the General Officer range serving in the three main theatres of war.

Each Division had its veterinary hospital administered by a Division-Veterinär. On the strength of each Regiment was a veterinary officer; and a *Ober-Veterinär* or *Veterinär* was permanently attached to each Cavalry Squadron or Artillery Troop.

General Oberst v. Einem wearing field-grey Kürassier uniform with coloured service cap.

The Plates

Plate A

In 1907 the General Staff experimented with a service dress to supplement the dress uniforms worn by the Army. A field-grey uniform was produced and issued to selected units for trial. It proved successful and was finally approved by Army Orders dated February 1910. It was basically the same cut for all Foot troops, Artillery and Train, but each arm of Cavalry retained a uniform which adhered to its own particular characteristics. Field-grey was selected for most arms, except Jäger, Schützen, Machine Gun units, Field Orderlies and Jäger zu Pferde, for which the colour green-grey was chosen. Coats had distinctive piping: Infantry and Machine Gun units, red; Jäger and Schützen, green; Artillery and Technical Services, scarlet;

Train, light blue; Pioneers, red; and the Prussian Guard Machine Gun unit, green, although permitted to retain black piping for collar and cuffs.

Field-grey tunics were fashioned with three types of cuff: the Brandenburg, with an oblong vertical flap fastened with three buttons; the Swedish, a round cuff with two buttons placed horizontally just below the top edge; and the Saxon, round like the Swedish, but with two buttons placed vertically by the back seam. Prussian Guard Schützen had Brandenburg cuffs but with three-pointed flaps. Shoulder strap buttons bore the company or squadron number in Arabic numerals. Other buttons had heraldic crowns. Shoulder straps were field-grey edged with coloured piping identifying the Army Corps. Prussian Guard and Baden Army Corps XIV infantry units had shoulder strap piping which corresponded with the colours of their dress uniforms: white, red, yellow and light blue, 5th Regiments white, and Guard Fusiliers lemon-yellow.

Army Corps	Shoulder Strap Piping
I, II, IX, X, XII (1st Saxon), and 1st Bavarian	White
III, IV, XI, XIII, XV, XIX (2nd Saxon) and 2nd Bavarian	Red
V, VI, XVI, XVII and 3rd Bavarian	Lemon-yellow
VII, VIII, XVIII and XX	Light blue
XXI	Light green

Guard and other distinguished regiments continued to wear traditional loops of lace (*litzen*) on collars and cuffs. This lace was of three types: double-bar, single-bar, and the type known as 'Old Prussian' pattern. Officers' lace was either gold or silver following the button colour; for other ranks the lace was white or yellow. NCOs wore strips of metallic (later grey) lace on collars and cuffs and had collar buttons:

Gefreite: A small button on each side of the collar.

Unteroffizier: Lace around the bottom of the collar and on the cuffs.

Feldwebel (*Wachtmeister* in Cavalry): As Unteroffizier, plus a large collar button.

Vizefeldwebel (*Etatsmässigefeldwebel*) (*Etatsmässige-wachtmeister*): As above, with additional band of lace above each cuff.

Offizierstellvertreter: As Vizefeldwebel with metallic braid around shoulder straps and metal unit designations.

Fähnrich: As Unteroffizier but with officers' sword-knot (Portepee).

Unteroffizier and Feldwebel wore the NCOs' pattern bayonet or swordknot, NCO ranks above this wore officers' swordknots (Portepee). Senior NCOs permitted portepees were entitled to wear officers' style cockades. Collar buttons were embellished with heraldic devices identifying the State: Prussia = eagle; Bavaria = lion; Saxony = arms; Württemberg = arms; Hesse = crown and shield. One year volunteers

Leutnant Rackow, commander, 1st Company, 158th Infantry Regiment (7th Lotheringian, König No. 7), holder of the *Pour le mérite*. This shows the full marching order of an infantry officer in the opening phase of the war. (R. G. Harris Collection)

Left:
Landsturmann of Landsturm Infantry Battalion No. 22. The unit and corps number are on either side of the collar front in Arabic and Roman numerals. Although the pouches are of the modern pattern, the rifle and bayonet are obsolete. The Landwehr Cross can be seen on the helmet cover above the unit number.

Centre:
An Artillery officer wearing the 'litewka'; the collar patches are black and piped around the edges with scarlet. (R. G. Harris Collection)

Right:
Infantryman of Reserve Infantry Regiment No. 239 in full marching order, 1914. Across the root of his shoulder strap is a coloured strip of cloth, which was a distinguishing mark peculiar to some divisions but not regulation.

(Freiwilligen) continued to wear twisted coloured cord in State colours around their shoulder straps. All officer grades wore shoulder cords which are described in the text for Plate D. Full dress headdress continued to be worn with covers. Infantry units had red numerals on the front of the covers, Reserve Regiments had 'R' over the numerals, and Landwehr units, a cross. After August 1914, numerals were altered to green.

Figure 1 is a trooper of the 3rd Brandenburg Hussar Regiment. His busby is worn with a cover. He wears the field-grey version of the dress '*atilla*' with the addition of pockets in the sides of the skirts. All braiding is field-grey, but rosettes on the rear of the skirts, rank buttons worn by NCOs and side hooks for the belt are blackened brass. Toggle fastenings, shoulder cord buttons and pocket buttons are grey horn. Rosettes of the breast looping are formed of the ends of the braiding itself and are not separate entities, as worn on the dress '*atilla*'. Shoulder cords are the colour of the dress '*atilla*' flecked with colour of the dress tunic braid. Field-grey breeches are trimmed with field-grey braid on the leg seams. Tunics of hussar officers were cut similarly to their peacetime '*Interim Atilla*' (undress tunic), all braiding being flecked with black thread. Regimental numbers or cyphers on shoulder cords were gilded; but peacetime shoulder belts, sash and sabretaches were not worn. Grey opossum fur busbies were worn uncovered by officers except for the 17th Regiment, who wore busbies made from brown bearskin and covered. Officers' breeches were field-grey and similar to those worn by their men. Officers generally wore brown leather lace-up boots with brown leather gaiters.

Figure 2 is a grenadier of the 1st Prussian Guard 'Kaiser Alexander Grenadier Regiment'. His tunic has Guard lace on the collar and Brandenburg cuff flaps. Guard Regiments did not have numerals on helmet covers. The bayonet tassel identifies him as serving with the 9th Company of the 3rd Battalion. He wears 1909-pattern infantry equipment with each cartridge pouch carrying twenty rounds of ammunition. Visible above his shoulders is the overcoat, strapped to the calfskin knapsack with a brown waterproof tent quarter folded on top.

Figure 3 is a Second Lieutenant of the 1st Prussian Foot Guards. Officers' lace is a silver 'double-bar' pattern. The coat and Swedish cuffs are piped red and the shoulder straps have a white underlay identifying the 1st Regiment.

Figure 4 is a Trooper of the 2nd Prussian Guard Machine Gun Detachment. The green-grey colour of the tunic is distinctly different from the field-grey worn by other troops. The broad brown leather belt with large steel rings hanging at the right hip is the harness belt used to drag machine guns over rough ground. The covered headdress is a shako of Jäger pattern made of grey-green cloth with brown leather top and visor and a brown leather chin strap. The headdress had the 'national' cockade on the right side, the Prussian cockade on the left and a Guard Star plate, silvered and enamelled for officers. Officers of the unit had gold lace set on green velvet collar patches.

Plate B

Figure 1 shows a Kürassier of the 3rd Regiment in the field service tunic which had distinctive braid for each regiment on collars and cuffs. Their coats had facing colour collar patches and cuffs. Coats were also piped with facing colour on collars, cuffs and down the front edges, along the bottoms and on the pocket flaps in the rear of the skirts. The Gardes du Corps and the Prussian Guard Regiment had collars and cuffs decorated with Guard lace and had additional piping along the bottom edges of the cuffs. NCOs had a central strip of metallic lace on

the collar and cuff braid. Officers' braid was figured grey silk with four raised ribs along its length and broad outer stripes in facing colour silks. Shoulder straps for other ranks were field-grey, piped with the facing colour, with an inner piping of white. Gardes du Corps and the Guard Regiment had plain straps, the remainder numerals or devices in red. Buttons were tombak for the 1st, 5th, 6th and 8th Regiments, and nickel for the Gardes du Corps, Guard Regiment and 2nd, 3rd, 4th and 7th Regiments. Undress caps were field-grey with cap bands in the facing colour piped with white. Grey cavalry breeches were worn with long brown jackboots.

Bavarian heavy cavalry regiments wore single-breasted, field-grey tunics with red piping on the top and fronts of the collars, the fronts of their coats and the rear skirt pockets. They had Swedish cuffs and field-grey shoulder straps piped red, with red numerals. The 1st Regiment had nickel, the 2nd Regiment tombak buttons. These regiments continued to wear pre-war dark grey overcoats. Leather equipment was brown.

Saxon heavy cavalry wore similar uniforms to Prussian kürassiers. The facing colour of the Guard Regiment was white and the Carabinier Regiment

A group of infantry in full marching order, November 1914.

Left:
An excellent study of the walking-out dress of a young infantryman of the 76th Infantry (2nd Hanseatic).

Right:
The same unit in full marching order. Particularly note the bugler on the extreme left of the group photograph.

black. Field-grey undress caps for Bavarians had facing colour bands and piping; Saxons had facing colour bands with pale blue piping. Saxon shoulder straps were piped with facing colour with inner pipings of pale blue. The Guard Regiment had red cyphers.

Figure 2 is a trooper of the 5th Westphalian Ulan Regiment. The field-grey coats of Ulan Regiments were cut similarly to the dress '*ulanka*', except that they were furnished with pockets in the sides of the skirts and had field-grey, pear-shaped shoulder straps piped in the colour of the full dress epaulette 'field'; all other piping was as on the full dress coat. Three Prussian Guard Regiments and the 13th, 17th, 18th, 19th and 21st Regiments wore 'Guard lace' in yellow or white according to the button colour of the dress coats. One bar of lace was worn on the cuffs. Field-grey undress caps had cap bands and piping in the regimental facing colours; regiments with cornflower blue cap bands (12th to 16th Regiments) were piped white. Bavarian Chevauleger Regiments wore a similar uniform except that the tunic had Swedish cuffs, ordinary field-grey shoulder straps, and plastron fronts piped along the right edge only. All piping was in regimental facing colour. Undress caps had facing colour bands and piping.

Figure 3 is a trooper of the 6th Magdeburg Dragoon Regiment. On his left shoulder he wears a black, white and red sharpshooters' cord. Dragoon regiments wore field-grey, single-breasted tunics with standing collars and Swedish cuffs. Buttons were either nickel or tombak, corresponding with button colours of dress uniforms. Piping on collars, cuffs, front edges and skirt pockets was as on the dress tunic. Shoulder straps were field-grey with piping in regimental facing colour and red numerals or cyphers. Collars of Prussian Guard Regiments were made square at the front, as were those of the 23rd Dragoons. The 1st and 2nd Prussian Guard Regiments had yellow and white Guard lace on their collars and cuffs respectively; the 17th and 25th Regiments had yellow lace; the 18th and 23rd Regiments, white lace. This lace was double-bar pattern for the 23rd Regiment, single-bar for the 17th, 18th and 25th; officers' lace was silver or gold accordingly. The 13th to 16th Regiments had white pipings on collars and cuffs, and the 19th had white piping on shoulder straps only. Prussian Guard officers had their lace on cornflower blue patches edged red. Undress caps had facing colour bands and pipings. The 2nd Regiment retained the privilege of wearing the small Prussian Eagle badge between the cockades.

Plate C

This plate illustrates infantry uniforms worn in the transitional period during the first year of the war. *Figures 1 and 3* are infantrymen of the 76th (2nd Hanseatic) Hamburg Infantry Regiment, serving with the IX Army Corps. The grey overcoat was as worn in peacetime except that, on mobilization, shoulder straps were changed to grey with Army Corps piping to correspond with the tunics. Collar patches for infantry were red; NCO's patches were distinguished by narrow vertical strips of white tape with stripes in State colours, and senior NCOs had two strips. Regiments wearing lace on tunic collars and cuffs wore similar bars on overcoat collar patches. *Figure 3* wears a dark grey toque to protect the ears from frost; his bayonet tassel identifies him as belonging to the 7th Company of the 2nd Battalion.

Figure 4 is a Jäger of the 9th Lauernberg Battalion serving with the IX Army Corps. Jäger uniforms were green-grey with green piping. All Prussian battalions had red numerals except the Guard Battalion, and the 11th Hessian Battalion had a red crowned 'M'. The Prussian Guard Battalion had additional green piping along the bottom edge of their cuffs and yellow Guard lace with a green 'light'. Jäger headdress was a black leather shako with black leather chinstrap. The Guard Battalion wore a Guard Star plate; the two Saxon Battalions had special pattern shakos. There were two Bavarian Jäger Battalions and a Mecklenberg Battalion. Instead of the normal bayonet, Jägers carried a long, sword-like 'hirschfänger' with distinctive green knot.

Figure 5 is a private of the 55th (6th Westphalian) Infantry Regiment, which formed part of the VII Army Corps, and his bayonet knot identifies him as a member of the 6th Company of the 2nd Battalion.

Figure 6 is a private of the 8th Company of the 2nd Battalion of the 102nd Royal Saxon Infantry Regiment, which formed part of the XII Army Corps. He displays all the characteristics of Saxon infantry: the green and white cockade on his cap band, the broad shoulder straps, the triangular pockets in the rear of the skirts, and the round cuffs with vertical buttons.

Figure 2 is a Prussian infantryman wearing full marching order, during the first six months of the war. The field-grey, adjustable, slip-on cap band was an innovation to render coloured bands less conspicuous. The calfskin knapsack is the 1895 pattern, on which the 1910-pattern mess cans are strapped; they had a handle attached and contained a cup, and combination spoon and fork. The

tent quarter is carried on top. On the right hip, suspended from the waistbelt, is a brown canvas haversack to which the water bottle is clipped. On the left hip an entrenching tool is suspended in a leather case from the belt; over it is the M98 bayonet with coloured knot identifying the man as a member of the 7th Company of a 2nd Battalion.

Plate D

The Landsturm was originally intended as a locally raised Defence Force for service in the Homeland. It did not come under effective central control until after 1875, thereafter assuming more characteristics of the regular forces. The headdress was a Jäger type shako with State cockade and the Landwehr Cross. *Figure 1* is a Landsturmann of the 12th Ellwagen (Westphalian) Landsturm Battalion of XII Army Corps in 1915. He wears a 1910-pattern tunic with red pipings and the blue shoulder straps of Landsturm infantry units; Foot Artillery had yellow, Field Artillery, scarlet, and Pioneers, black straps. The Landsturm wore brass numerals on the collar fronts: the Army Corps identified by Roman numerals placed over Arabic numerals giving the battalion. Prussian Guard Landsturm units had a 'G' over the battalion numbers. Landsturm were generally armed and equipped with obsolete weapons and equipment.

Figure 2 is a Captain (*Hauptmann*) of the 9th Battalion, Prussian Train, wearing the 1910-pattern field service uniform. The arm of service colour of the Train was blue and their coats were piped red. The Captain wears silver, black-flecked shoulder cords on blue underlay. The flecking on officers' shoulder cords was in State Colours: black for Prussia, light blue for Bavaria, green for Saxony, black and red for Württemberg, etc. Second Lieutenants had plain cords, First Lieutenants one star, and Captains two stars. Majors, Lieutenant-Colonels and full Colonels had plaited silver cords, the former with plain straps, the latter with one and two stars respectively. General Officers wore gold and silver plaited cords; Major-Generals had plain straps, Lieutenant-Generals one star, full Generals two stars, and Colonel-Generals three stars. Field Marshals wore crossed batons. Unit numerals or cyphers were worn between the stars.

Figure 3 is a Captain serving on the Prussian

An NCO of the Guard Grenadier Regiment Königen Elizabeth, No. 3. Note the Guard 'litzen' on the collar and cuff flaps, also the NCO's braid around the collar and top of the cuffs. (R. G. Harris Collection)

appropriate colours were worn. Adjutants' sashes and the undress *'feldbinde'* ceased to be worn after 1915, the *'feldbinde'* being replaced by a leather waistbelt.

Figure 4. General officers wore field service tunics with breast pockets with flaps and 'Saxon' pockets in the rear of the skirts. Cuffs were deep and round. On each collar front generals wore scarlet patches decorated with distinctive gold embroidery known as *'Alt Larisch'* pattern. General-Adjutants wore similar tunics with Prussian Guard gold embroidered lace on the collar patches. General officers attached to the Kaiser's Suite wore similar pattern coats with silver lace and buttons. Flügel-Adjutants wore infantry pattern coats with silver lace of the same type as General-Adjutants; Adjutants to the Princes of the Royal Houses wore infantry pattern tunics with special distinctive silver lace on the collars. Trousers and breeches of Generals, Adjutants, Military Cabinet and War Ministry Staffs all had piping and broad stripes in the colour of their collar patches. The Train officer and General Officer both wear the *'feldbinde'*, a 5cm-wide undress belt made of silver woven thread with silk stripes of the State colour worked in. The clasps were in the button colour. Saxon generals had three light green stripes; Württemberg officers wore silver belts with two black/red stripes (one colour immediately above the other), Baden and Oldenberg officers wore silver belts with one narrow red stripe between two black stripes, Hessians silver belts with three red stripes, and Mecklenburg officers gold belts with a blue, a yellow and a red stripe. Devices on clasps differed in pattern from State to State.

Plate E

In the autumn of 1915 (March 1916 for Bavaria), the 1910-pattern field service uniform started to be replaced by a simpler field uniform. Transition was slow, and the 1910-pattern continued to be worn with modifications, the most significant being a simpler form of cuff. Early in 1916 a steel helmet was introduced to replace the leather *'picklehaube'*, which had proved inadequate. Some units continued to make do with the old pattern helmets, often with the spikes removed, and often a mixture was worn, even within one battalion. Units serving on the Eastern Front were among the last to be

General Staff. The Staff tunic had carmine collar patches, pipings and underlay. Officers of the General Staff and War Ministry Staff wore carmine piping with broad carmine stripes down the outside of each leg. An Adjutants' sash was worn over the right shoulder. Bavaria, Saxony and Württemberg each had its own General Staff and sashes in issued with the steel helmet.

Figure 1 is a Second Lieutenant of the 13th Foot Artillery Regiment. He wears an undress cap and the *'litewka'*. This undress coat was universally favoured by officers throughout the German Army. It was double-breasted with a low fold-over collar and deep round cuffs; the back was plain with a central vent. The collar had patches in distinctive colours, and piping down the front, on the edges of the collar and on the cuffs. Field Artillery had scarlet collar patches (with white piping outline for the 1st, yellow for the 3rd and pale blue for the 4th Prussian Guard Regiments). All artillery had yellow buttons. The Train had blue patches and red piping elsewhere on the coat; buttons were yellow for the 1st Guard unit and all line units, but white for the 2nd Guard. Infantry had white patches; Prussian Foot Guards' patches were piped white, red, yellow and pale blue, and yellow for the Guard Fusiliers; the 5th Foot Guards and 5th Guard Grenadier Regiment had no piping. Piping on the coat was red for Infantry. Officers' shoulder cords were underlaid with the colour of the full dress shoulder straps for the Guard, and white for the remainder of the infantry. The 8th Prussian Grenadier Regiment had red-piped patches, the 109th Regiment white, the 114th Regiment pale green, the 7th Grenadier Regiment yellow, the 11th Grenadier Regiment yellow and the 145th Regiment dark blue patch piping. Jäger Battalions had green collar patches and red coat piping; Pioneers, black patches piped red, and red coat piping; Specialist Troops, grey patches, the Aeroplane Units with patches piped white, red, yellow and light blue in sequence for the 1st, 2nd, 3rd and 4th Battalions.

Figure 2 in the rear is a Gefreite of the 110th Baden Reserve Grenadier Regiment. He wears the old style helmet with spike removed, and his coat is a modified version of the 1910 tunic with plain round cuffs. Numerals on the shoulder straps are covered with grey slip-on tabs.

Figure 4 depicts a Gunner of the 2nd Troop, 5th Battery, 21st Field Artillery Regiment. He wears a covered ball-mounted artillery helmet with 1915 field blouse, and black leather equipment with obsolete M1889-pattern cartridge pouches. The brown leather cavalry-pattern swordknot strap and coloured tassel identify his troop and battery.

Figure 3 is an Unteroffizier of the 63rd (4th Silesian) Infantry Regiment. He wears the 1915 blouse with arm of service piping on the shoulder straps and red regimental numerals. The NCO collar lace is a modified, simpler type, as used on the blouse; he wears cloth puttees and ankle boots instead of marching boots.

Figure 5 wears the new pattern 1916 steel shrapnel helmet. An NCO Specialist of the Prussian Guard Reserve Pioneer Regiment, his blouse has Guard lace on the collar. On the left cuff he wears a black circular badge with a 'death's-head', the distinction of a flamethrower (Flammenwerfer) detachment. These troops also formed part of the Assault Troops (see Plate H).

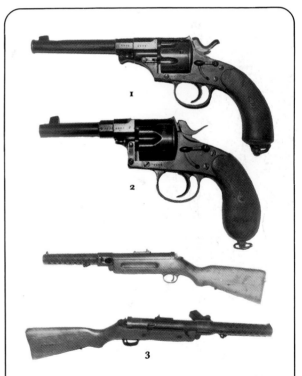

Three of the least well-known weapons used by the German Army during World War I: (1) The Reichs Revolver M/79 Cavalry Model, issued to artillery drivers and reserve units; calibre 10·55mm. (2) The Reichs Revolver M/79 Infantry Officers' Model, and issued to reserve units; 10·55mm calibre. (3) The MP (Machinepistole) 18 I Bergmann; 9mm calibre, weighing 4kg. Introduced during the summer of 1918 on the Western Front and used mainly by special formations and assault troops. It had a drum magazine holding 32 rounds and was issued to all officers, NCOs, and ten men from each assault company. In infantry companies it was issued to 6 men who formed a 'Machinepistole Truppe'. (Imperial War Museum)

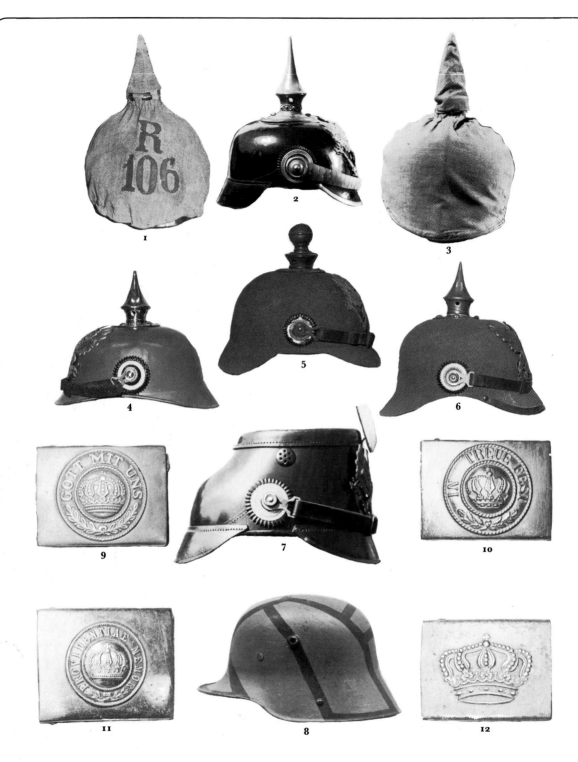

(1–6): Types of picklehaube worn during World War I. The top row shows the leather helmet with and without an other ranks' field-grey cover for Reserve Infantry Regiment No. 106 (3) Officers' cover (4) Pressed-steel version (5, 6) Pressed-felt versions (7) Jäger shako (8) 1916-pattern trench Stahlhelme complete with camouflage paintwork (9, 10) Belt plates of Prussia and Baden, and Bavaria (11, 12) Belt plates of Saxony, and Hesse. The belt plates of Württemberg bore the State coat of arms and the motto *Furchtlos und Treu.* (Imperial War Museum)

Plate F

Besides colonial troops (Schütztruppen) Germany had provided her Marine Infantry and troops of the 1905 East Asian Occupation Brigade with a lightweight hot weather clothing, in both grey and brown drill. Headdresses for these troops comprised grey felt spiked helmets; another version covered in drill with bronze fittings; brown or white tropical helmets; and the distinctive grey slouch hats of the regular colonial forces, plus normal undress caps, including a version made from brown drill. Regular colonial troops serving in the old German colonies continued to wear their normal tropical clothing, but regular German forces sent to theatres of war in Palestine, Sinai, Bulgaria and Greece were issued with khaki drill uniform, or had normal uniforms modified for hot weather conditions. Little is known about the hot weather uniforms issued to troops serving in Palestine but photographs suggest they wore tropical helmets in brown drill without the eagle plates worn by regular colonial troops. In its place, worn on the helmet band, was a large national cockade. Bands were white for infantry, or black piped red for artillery. Von Sandars, commander of the German forces in Palestine, issued orders for the tropical helmet to be replaced by the brown drill cap to avoid confusion with British troops who wore similar headdress. Brown drill jackets were fashioned with turned-down collars, breast and hip pockets and were fastened by six metal buttons. Infantry had either plain shoulder straps, or straps piped with Army Corps colours with red numerals; Artillery had scarlet piping and red grenades or numerals; Train had blue piping, and Medical troops dark blue piping. Trousers were the same colour as the jacket and worn with dark grey or brown puttees and brown leather ankle boots. Soft drill caps were worn with neck curtains of the same material. Caps were fashioned with brown peaks and chinstraps. Cap bands were plain drill for Infantry; black piped red for Artillery, and blue piped red for Train.

Figure 1 is an infantryman, *Figure 2* an artilleryman serving in Palestine. *Figure 3* is a private of the 1st Masurian Infantry Regiment which also served in Palestine. The three figures on the right represent German troops serving in the Macedonian campaign in 1917. *Figure 4* is an Ulan of

Officer of a Guard Grenadier Regiment wearing a waistbelt with bayonet frog and bayonet. The swordknot is worn as the men would have worn the *troddeln* and can be seen below the bottom of the skirt hem.

the 6th Thuringian Regiment. He wears the normal field-grey service dress with lance cap covered in dust-coloured material and a neck curtain. In 1915, the pear-shaped shoulder straps were gradually replaced by normal-shaped red straps with yellow cyphers or numerals. *Figure 5* is a trooper of a Mountain Machine Gun Battery wearing a '*picklehaube*' of pressed felt with spike removed; this headdress is also provided with a neck curtain. Mountain troops wore puttees and special climbing boots and often had their uniforms reinforced with leather at elbow and knee. *Figure 6* is a Jäger of the Prussian Guard Battalion. He wears the 1915 blouse, the collar decorated with Guard lace. The 1916-pattern steel helmet is covered with sacking and he carries the all-green bayonet knot. Campaigning in the mountainous regions of Macedonia was particularly rigorous and German sources emphasize the patched and makeshift nature of the uniforms worn by all ranks. Photographs suggest that mixtures of field-grey and drill uniforms were also worn by all ranks in Palestine.

Plate G

Figure 1 represents an officer of the Württemberg Ski Company. The headdress closely resembles the

A clear study of the field-grey service uniform of a General Officer. (R. Marrion Collection)

cap worn by the Austrian Army. It had two small buttons on the front, the National Cockade on the right side and the State Cockade on the left. It was piped all round the crown with green. The special field-grey tunic had the collar piped green and was fashioned with two green-piped pockets in the rear of the skirts, each fastened with two buttons; it also had two breast pockets and two hip pockets. On the collar fronts were grey patches bearing a green 'S'. Company medical officers had blue collar patches, piped red with red 'S' thereon. Tunics worn by other ranks were without shoulder straps. Men were equipped with brown leather waistbelts, cartridge pouches without braces, skis, M98 cavalry carbines and bayonets. Officers' shoulder cords were silver, flecked red and black, on a green underlay.

Figure 2 shows an officer of the Württemberg Mountain Battalion. The uniform closely resembles the Ski Company dress, except for green collar patches with yellow metal buttons towards the rear. In addition, other ranks had green woollen 'rolls' at the tops of the sleeves on the shoulder seams, after the Austrian fashion. On active service the battalion wore the mountain cap as in Figure 1, but alternatively could wear shakos with covers. These units fought with distinction in Rumania, the Balkans and in Italy. Erwin Rommel was a company commander in the Mountain Battalion.

Figure 3 is an officer of the Prussian Guard-Schützen Battalion wearing the new Walking Out uniform prescribed by Prussian Cabinet Order of 21 September 1915, giving a new dimension to the field-grey uniform, offsetting the plain 1915 field blouse. The uniform was not issue but optional, and was purchased at their own expense by officers and men. Details of all variations of this uniform are too complex to describe here, but briefly it comprised a field-grey tunic with a standing collar, worn with dark-grey trousers, and a field-grey, grey-visored cap, for all ranks (see Table I).

Kürassiers wore tunics with collar patches, cuffs and piping, including piping up the back seams of the coat, in regimental facing colour and collars and cuffs trimmed with regimental braid. Ulans wore an '*ulanka*' with facing colour collar and cuffs; plastron piping and piping up the back seams of the coat were also in the facing colour. Shoulder straps were plain red with yellow numerals or

TABLE I

Arm	Collar	Cuffs	Cuff Flaps	Piping	Shoulder Straps	Numerals and Devices
Infantry	Red	Red	Red	Red	Field-grey (1)	Red
Jäger and Schützen (2)	Green	Green	Nil	Green	Green	Red
Gd-Schützen	Black	Black	Grey-green	Green	Green	Red
Pioneers	Black	Black	Nil	Red	Black	Red
Technical Troops	Black	Black	Nil	Red	Field-grey	Red
Field Artillery	Black	Black	Nil	Scarlet	Scarlet	Yellow
Foot Artillery	Black	Black	Field-grey (3)	Scarlet	Yellow	Red
Train	Blue	Blue	Nil	Blue	Blue	Red
Medical Troops	Dark blue	Dark blue	Field-grey	Dark blue	Dark blue	Yellow
Jäger z.Pferde (4)	Green	Green	Nil	Regimental Facing colour	Green	Red
Dragoons	Facing colour	Facing colour	Nil	Facing colour	Cornflower blue	Red

(1) Guard Infantry had white shoulder straps piped with the colour of the full dress tunic shoulder strap; line infantry had white piping on the shoulder straps.

(2) Jäger, Schützen, Guard-Schützen and Jäger, and Jäger zu Pferde wore green-grey tunics.

(3) Guard Foot Artillery did not have cuff flaps.

(4) Jäger zu Pferde had collars and cuffs trimmed with regimental braid.

TABLE II

Arm	Body Colour	Cap Band	Pipings
Infantry	Field-grey	Red	Red
Jäger	Grey-green	Green	Green
Schützen	Grey-green	Black	Green
Pioneers	Field-grey	Black	Red
Artillery (all grades)	Field-grey	Black	Scarlet
Specialist Troops	Field-grey	Black	Red
Train	Field-grey	Blue	Blue
Medical Troops	Field-grey	Dark blue	Dark blue
Cavalry:			
Kürassiers (1)	White	Regimental facing colour	Regimental facing colour
Dragoons	Cornflower blue	Regimental facing colour	Regimental facing colour
Ulans	Field-grey	Regimental facing colour	Regimental facing colour
Jäger zu Pferde	Grey-green	Regimental facing colour	Regimental facing colour
General Officers	Field-grey	Scarlet	Scarlet

(1) All ranks of Kürassiers also had a field-grey cap with band in regimental facing and white piping. Hussars wore caps similar to their full dress caps with grey visors and chinstraps.

devices. Hussars wore a field-grey 'atilla' with grey collar and cuffs and shoulder cords in the colour of the full dress 'atilla' flecked with colour of the braid. The Life Guard Hussar Regiment wore their full dress 'atilla'. Officers' lace and embroidery, Guard lace and other regimental distinctions were allowed on this dress. Officers as an alternative wore the 'Kleine rock', or 'litewka' with service dress shoulder cords, not epaulettes. All ranks were permitted a service cap with a grey visor and chinstrap in the following colours (see Table II).

Dark grey trousers were worn with this uniform,

TABLE III

Arm	Rank and File	Officers:	
		Trousers	Gala hose
Infantry	Red	Red	Red
Jäger and Schützen	Green	Green	Green (1)
Pioneers	Red	Red	Red (2)
Artillery	Scarlet	Scarlet	Scarlet (3)
Specialist Troops	Red	Red	Red (3)
Train	Red	Red	Blue
Medical	Red	Red	No Gala hose
Kürassiers	Red (a)	Red (a)	(4)
Dragoons	Red (b)	Red (b)	(5)
Ulans	Red	Red	(6)
Hussars	(7)	(7)	No Gala hose (7)
Jäger zu Pferde	Green	Green	(8)
Generals	(9)	(9)	(9)

(1) Guard-Schützen green piping, black velvet stripes piped green on the outer edges.

(2) (3) Red or scarlet piping, black stripes with red or scarlet piping down the outside edges.

(4) A stripe of gold or silver lace (according to the button colour) down the outside of each leg edged on either side with the facing colour. Gardes du Corps and Guard Regt had white gala hose.

(5) Piping and very broad stripes in the facing colour: 6th, 11th and 12th Regts in velvet; 22nd, red piping and black stripes piped red.

(6) 1st Guard Regt, scarlet piping and white stripes.

(7) Hussars wore dark grey riding breeches. Officers gold or silver, rank and file yellow or white stripes according to the button colour.

(8) Silver or gold lace stripe edged with facing colour according to the button colour.

(9) Generals wore scarlet piping and scarlet stripes on trousers, gala hose or breeches.

(a) 5th Regt pink, 2nd Regt crimson.

(b) 3rd and 7th Regts pink, 15th rose, 11th and 12th crimson stripes.

---

with piped outer seams. Officers could wear 'gala hose'—dark grey trousers with piping and a broad stripe each side of it (see Table III).

Plate H

Owing to the specialized nature of their duties, uniforms and equipment of Assault Troops underwent modifications. In the early months ammunition pouches were discarded, ammunition being carried in tunic pockets. Later, three pouches were carried on one side of the belt with a trench knife on the other. Puttees were worn with lace-up ankle boots, patches of leather reinforced elbows and knees of clothing, and equipment was reduced to greatcoats rolled and strapped around mess tins. Special weapons were devised for trench fighting, varying from clubs to all types of modified bayonets and knives; most readily available and easily adaptable was the entrenching tool with sharpened edges. Men of assault detachments were called 'grenadiers'.

Officially special insignia was frowned on, but there are records of badges being worn. One group photograph shows members of an assault unit wearing a dark-coloured cloth grenade on the left upper sleeve. Men of the Assault Company, 23rd Saxon (1st Saxon) Reserve Division attached to XII Army Corps wore a green brassard on the left arm, edged with white and with a white 'S' in the centre. The few official Specialist insignia included a 'death's-head' patch for Flamethrower Detachments and the 'MW' initials worn on the shoulder straps of Trench Mortar (Minenwerfer) personnel. White smocks with hoods were worn when attacks were made over snow-covered ground.

Figures 1 and 2 are wearing the blouse, *Figure 3 and 4* modified 1910 tunics. The blouse (*'Bluse'*) was introduced in 1915. It dispensed with lavish pipings and cuff distinctions for all arms and services. It was a simple, field-grey, single-breasted coat; buttons down the front were covered with a fly. Coats were made with green or field-grey turn-down collars and simple, deep turn-back cuffs. The rear of the coats had single vents with two hook-buttons at the waist, plus one hook each side to support the waistbelts. On the sides of the skirts were pockets with flaps and buttons. Trousers were issued in the same colour as the blouse. Jäger and Schützen units retained distinctive green-grey uniforms but Machine Gun units now wore field-grey. Distinctive 1910-pattern cavalry tunics were also gradually replaced by blouses, particularly on the Western Front. Unit identification was confined to shoulder straps, although regiments entitled to lace distinctions still wore them on the collars only. NCOs' braid was also simplified, placed only on the front and the first few centimetres along the bottom of the collar; cuff braid was restricted to a short bar at the top of the cuff. The peacetime greatcoat was gradually replaced by a field-grey universal pattern for all arms and ranks, with shoulder straps as worn on the blouse. Leather equipment was blackened and black universal cavalry boots were introduced.

Shoulder strap colours on the *'Bluse'* were as follows (see Table IV):

TABLE IV

Army of Service	Cloth	Piping	Numeral or Cypher
Infantry	Field-grey	White (1)	Red
Jäger and Schützen	Green-grey	Light green (2)	Red
Artillery—Foot	Golden yellow	None (3)	Red
Artillery—Horse and Field	Scarlet	None	Lemon-yellow
Pioneers	Black	Scarlet	Red
Communication Troops	Light grey	None	Red
Train	Blue	None	Red
Medical	Dark blue	Cornflower blue	Yellow
Stretcher Bearers	Crimson	None	Yellow
Cavalry:			
Kürassiers	White	As on 1910 tunics	Golden yellow (a)
Dragoons	Cornflower blue	As on 1910 tunics (4)	Red (b)
Hussars	Cords: as on 1910 field-grey atilla	Not applicable	Yellow or white (c)
Lancers	Scarlet	As on 1910 tunics (5)	Lemon-yellow
Jäger zu Pferde	Light green	As on 1910 tunics (6)	Red (d)
Bavarian Heavy Cavalry	Field-grey	As on 1910 tunics	Red
Bavarian Chevauleger Regts	Field-grey	As on 1910 tunics	Red
Saxon Heavy Cavalry	Field-grey	As on 1910 tunics	Red (e)

(1) Except 2nd Ft Gds, 2nd Gd Grenadiers and 8th Grenadiers, which are red; 3rd Ft Gds, 3rd Guard Grenadiers, Guard Fusiliers, 7th and 11th Grenadiers, which are lemon-yellow; 4th Ft Gds, 4th Guard Grenadiers, 145th Inf. Regt, which are light blue; and 114th Inf. Regt, which is light green.

(2) Except Guard Schützen Battalion, which is black.

(3) Except 1st Guard Field Artillery Regt, which is white; 3rd Guard Field Artillery Regt, lemon-yellow; and 4th Guard Field Artillery Regt, light blue.

(4) Except 22nd Dragoons, which is black only.

(5) No scarlet piping for the 2nd Guard Ulans, 2nd, and 6th Ulans.

(6) The piping for the newly formed 9th, 10th, 11th, 12th and 13th Regts is identical with that of the 2nd, 3rd, 4th, 5th and 6th Regts. The 7th Regt had pink piping.

(a) Crimson for the 2nd Kürassiers.

(b) Except for the 3rd Horse Grenadiers and the 7th and 15th Dragoons, which are pink; and the 11th and 12th Dragoons, which are crimson.

(c) White for the 4th, 6th, 7th, 9th, 10th and 17th Hussars, remainder golden-yellow. The 1st Leib-Hussars wear the Imperial Cypher.

(d) Except for the 1st Regt, which is lemon-yellow, and the 7th which is pink.

(e) Red for the Guard Regt only.

Landsturm Formations had the shoulder straps of their 1915-pattern blouses in the following colours: Infantry = blue; Field Artillery = scarlet; Foot Artillery = yellow; Pioneers = black. Metal numerals were retained on the collar fronts as on the earlier pattern tunics.

INDEX

(References to illustrations are shown in **bold**. Plates are shown with caption locators in brackets.)

Air Service 24–25
Anti-Aircraft Machine-Gun detachments 23
Army Corps Districts 11–12
artillery 12–16 *see also* weapons
artillery officer **28**
artilleryman, Mountain Artillery Battery No. 2: **21**
assault troops 18–19, **23**, **H1–H4** (38–39)
Ausmarch, 1914: 7–8

Baden Reserve Grenadier Rgt., 110th **E2** (32–33)
balloon units 24, 25
Bavarian Assault Battalion **H1** (38–39)
belt-plates **34**
body armour, trench **21**, **23**
Brandenburg Hussar Rgt., 3rd **A1** (26–29)
Bridging Trains 24
buttons, collar 27–28 *see also* insignia

captains **D2**, **D3** (31–32)
cavalry 19–20, 23
Cavalry, 76th (2nd Hanseatic) **30**
cavalry trooper, 1st Saxon Reiter Regiment **16**
clothing, lightweight hot weather 35
coats **6**, **28**, 33
Communication troops 25
conscription 9–10
Construction Officers, Fortress 24
corps commanders 8
corps strength, 1914: 9
cuffs 27, **37** *see also* insignia
cyclist troops 17–18, 23

driver, Field Artillery unit **14**

Einem, General Oberst v. **26**
Einjahrige Freiwilligen (one year volunteers) 10
Engineers, Corps of 24
Ersatz (supplementary) Reserve 10

Field Artillery 12, 13–14
    21st Rgt. **E4** (32–33)
Foot Artillery 12–13, 14–15
    13th Rgt. **E1** (32–33)
Fortress Construction Officers 24
'Freikorps' 7
Fusilier Regiment, 40th **10**

gefreite, 110th Baden Reserve Grenadier Rgt.
    E2 (32–33)
general officers **D4** (31–32), **36**
grenadier, 1st Prussian Guard 'Kaiser Alexander
    Grenadier Rgt.' **A2** (26–29)
Guard Grenadier Regiments 19, **32**
gunners 14, **E4** (32–33)

Hamburg Inf. Rgt., 76th (2nd Hanseatic) **C1**,
    C3 (30–31)
headgear **19**, 28–29, 32–33, **34**, 35, **37**
Hussars, 11th (2nd Westphalian) **17**

infantry **9**, 16–18, **18**, **21**, **28**, **29**, **30**, **F1**, **F2** (35–36),
    H3 (38–39)
Infantry Rgt., 55th (6th Westphalian) **C5** (30–31)
Infantry Rgt., 63rd (4th Silesian) **E3** (32–33)
insignia 26–39, **37**, **39**

Jäger Battalions 17, 18, **C4** (30–31), **F6** (35–36)

Kürassier patrol **22**
Kürassier Rgt., 3rd **B1** (29–30)

lace loops 27 *see also* insignia
Landsturm (Home Guard) **4**, 9–10, 11, **28**,
    D1 (31–32)
Landsturm Bn., 12th Ellwagen (Westphalian)
    D1 (31–32)
Lauernberg, 9th, Jäger Bn. **C4** (30–31)
lieutenants, 2nd **A3** (26–29), **E1** (32–33),
    G1–G3 (36–38)

machine-gun units 11, 12, 20–23
Magdeburg Dragoon Rgt., 6th **B3** (29–30)
Masurian Inf. Rgt., 1st **F3** (35–36)
medical officer **8**
Medical Service 26
Mining Companies 24
mobilisation 10–12
Moltke, Helmuth Karl Bernhard, Graf von 3
Mountain Artillery 12–13, 15
Mountain Machine Gun Battery **F5** (35–36)
Musketen Battalions 23

NCOs **3**, **7**, **32**, **E5** (32–33), **H1**, **H2** (38–39)

officers **28**, 35, 36 **D4**, (31–32)
organisation 8–9

Pioneers, Corps of **13**, **14**, 24
piping 26–27, **37**, **39** *see also* insignia
privates **6**, **C1–C3**, **C5**, **C6** (30–31), **F1–F3** (35–36),
    H4 (38–39)
Prussian Foot Guards, 1st **A3** (26–29)
Prussian General Staff **D3** (31–32)
Prussian Guard, 1st, 'Kaiser Alexander Grenadier
    Rgt.' **A2** (26–29)
Prussian Guard, 2nd, Machine Gun Detachment
    A4 (26–29)
Prussian Guard Corps 11, **E5** (32–33), **F6** (35–36),
    G3 (36–38)

Prussian Inf. Rgt. **C2** (30–31)
Prussian Train, 9th Bn. **D2** (31–32)
Rackow, Leutnant **27**
Railway Service 25
regiments 7–8
Reserve Infantry Regiment No. 239: **28**
Restanten Liste 10
rifleman, 10th Jäger Battalion **21**
Rohr, Hauptmann Ulrich 19

Saxon (1st Saxon) Reserve Division, 23rd
    H4 (38–39)
Saxon Inf. Rgt., 102nd Royal **C6** (30–31)
Saxon Reiter Regiment, 1st **16**, **20**
Schlieffen, Albrecht, Graf von 4
Schlieffen Plan 4–5
shoulder straps 27, 28, **37**, **39** *see also* insignia
Signals Service 25
Ski Battalions 18
specialist units 17
Sturmbataillone 18–19
Sturmbataillon, 5th, 'Rohr' **H2** (38–39)
Sturmkompanie 18–19

Telegraph troops 25
Thuringian Ulan Rgt., 6th **F4** (35–36)
Train Battalion 16
transport 18
Transport Service, Mechanical 25–26
trench warfare 5, **10**
troopers **A1**, **A4** (26–29), **B1–B3** (29–30), **F4**,
    F5 (35–36)
tropical clothing 35
trousers **38**

Uechtritz und Steinkirch, General-
    major v. **15**
Ulan patrol **5**
uniforms 26–39, **37**, 38
unteroffizier, 63rd (4th Silesian) Inf. Rgt. **E3** (32–33)

Veterinary Services 26

walking-out dress **30**, **G3** (36–38)
weapons 33
    field howitzers 13
    machine-gun 22–23
    MP18 I Bergmann **33**
    pistol, long artillery **21**
    Reichs revolver 33
Westphalian Ulan Rgt., 5th **B2** (29–30)
Wilhelm, Kaiser 6
Württemberg, 2nd, König Wilhelm **3**
Württemberg Battalions 18, **G1**, **G2** (36–38)